generating context

THE PRACTICE OF PERRY DEAN ROGERS | PARTNERS ARCHITECTS

generating context

MICHAEL J. CROSBIE

BIRKHÄUSER | PUBLISHERS FOR ARCHITECTURE
BASEL • BERLIN • BOSTON

Book Design: Hecht Design, Arlington, Massachusetts

A CIP catalogue record for this book is available from the Library of Congress,
Washington D.C., USA

Deutsche Bibliothek Cataloging–in–Publication Data

Crosbie, Michael J.:
Generating Context : The Practice of Perry Dean Rogers|Partners Architects / Michael J. Crosbie.
–Basel; Berlin; Boston : Birkhäuser, 2001
    ISBN 3–7643–6438–6

© 2001 Birkhäuser – Publishers for Architecture, P.O. Box 133, CH-4010 Basel, Switzerland
A member of the BertelsmannSpringer Publishing Group
Printed on acid-free paper produced from chlorine-free pulp. TCF
Printed in Germany
ISBN 3–7643–6438–6
9 8 7 6 5 4 3 2 1

CONTEXT AND COLLABORATION

Perry Dean Rogers | Partners Architects' approach to architecture is complex, mature, and provocative. Founded in 1923 as Perry Shaw and Hepburn, the office is multigenerational and builds upon its own history. The office's work is the product not of one lead designer, or of self-contained studios under one roof. Rather, multiple talents of different ages collaborate in myriad ways. There is a great deal of borrowing and melding of ideas, which are invented anew and interpreted in refreshing ways. I think this methodology of practice is what keeps the work both balanced and innovative.

The office approaches each commission with a clear set of convictions. First, they analyze needs and generate solutions by enfranchising the client and users in the design process. They remain open and engaged with clients and their needs. They search for solutions to architectural problems that address and emphasize those client needs. And they create architecture that invites its users to see the world in a fresh way. Perry Dean Rogers and Partners attracts clients who are empathetic with the architects' goals.

One of the architectural practices most important to the firm, and the focus of this book, is academic work. All of the projects in this book are academic buildings, but they represent a wide range and offer nearly every type of design problem that one might encounter. There are libraries, an office of admissions, visual arts centers and a theater, student unions and campus centers, a computer center, dormitories, classroom buildings, faculty offices, and entire campus plans.

Clients in academia, those who administer colleges and universities, research institutes, and private schools, tend to take a long view regarding large capital investments such as buildings. They build with a sense of stewardship. They will be the principal users of what they build,

they build to enhance the value and standing of their institutions, and they usually act with a deep awareness of the institution's history. They know that the decisions made about a building's design and its placement on a campus are lasting ones, and that those who come after will tend to be unforgiving of the mistakes of those who have built before.

Certainly, the plethora of academic clients over the decades has been key to the firm's interest in context. A sensitivity to context seems to be a prerequisite to responsible campus design. Campuses are, for the most part, small, self-contained worlds. They are affected far more dramatically by a new building than cities would be. On a campus, context matters because every new building has the potential to change it greatly.

Virtually all buildings have an existing built context (except, perhaps, buildings on remote sites, but even they have the greater context of other buildings in the region). Today, architects exhibit the full gamut of responses to context. A large number of practitioners simply choose to ignore it, and design and build whatever they wish, or what they are compelled to by their clients. Others seem so enthralled by context that it becomes a prison. Those architects seem to believe that responding to context absolves them of a rigorous pursuit of exemplary design.

Another influence on Perry Dean Rogers and Partners' interest in context is the city in which they are based. Boston has a rich building heritage, layers of built history, and a culture that values architecture. Boston's cultural setting, I believe, imparts a certain interest in and respect for previous building traditions. It is a culture that architects absorb, either consciously or unconsciously, and they become attuned to the influence of context.

Perry Dean Rogers and Partners approaches context as an ethic, the principles of which extend beyond the built reality. First, they understand that the circumstances of every project are

unique to that project. They take into account the history of the place, buildings that may have been there once and are now forever gone. Context includes the institution's image of itself, its place in the constellation of institutions of higher learning. Context describes the patterns of human habitation as they are right now at a variety of scales (the classroom, the building, the campus, the institution, the world beyond) and how they might change through design. Context includes the conditions one finds in how people use space, how they move across the campus, and how they view the institution and themselves.

Context is also understood to be evolutionary, unfolding, and transforming over time. Therefore, contextual considerations extend beyond the built reality and the considerations of site to include our place in time. Beyond this, Perry Dean Rogers and Partners includes the shared memories of those in the academic community, using its buildings to reinforce, comment upon, or call into question that shared history.

An existing situation can be considered the generator of a new building. The context is a surrounding milieu, buildings and culture, within which a new work originates, develops, and is contained. Ultimately, building and context produce one another. Perry Dean Rogers and Partners believes that it is vital to a community that a new work of architecture intimately connect with existing cultural, physical, and environmental conditions. It should be integrated into a place, flexible over time, and economically and environmentally sustainable. Inclusiveness is a hallmark of this approach, leading to design solutions that synthesize a combination of diverse elements. Taking such an approach to context requires willingness on the part of the architect to look deeply, to listen carefully, to include as many of these diverse elements in the design as possible.

One manifestation of this is how the firm chooses to work with clients. In 1974, Perry Dean Rogers and Partners developed the award-winning "Wall Process," an information gathering, structuring, and prioritizing method, which has continued to develop and gain relevance over time as clients have embraced a more inclusive process. The Wall Process, so named for the surfaces covered with layers of sketches and notations for critique, offers a technique for collecting ideas from people throughout all levels of the institution. Blank sheets of paper record concerns, ideas, notions, needs, and wishes of those who will use the building or work in it. Later in the project, the wall displays schematic design ideas upon which critiques are made by the same audience. Such a technique, used in various forms in many of the office's projects, is not only an effective design influence; it also enfranchises those who will ultimately live with the built results.

Being influenced by a rich, inclusive base of context protects the building from becoming an exercise in formalism, an elaborate architectural game divorced from the concerns of those who will inhabit the built environment. Every building and project of the office manifests a consistently high level of care. Each reveals a penetrating engagement by its designers. Always there are the stitches that knit the architecture to what is there, and make it part of a much larger whole. Throughout, one finds the imprints of students, faculty, and administrators, echoes of what has come before, and hints of where we might go next.

The following sections present 21 buildings and projects organized according to six themes prevalent in the firm's work. The first section, "Building Landscape," describes a condition in which building and landscape are woven together to the extent that there may be no clear definition of where one ends and the other begins. "Relative Objects," the subject of the second

section, are what result when design takes the measure of the buildings that are already there, and expands on existing systems. "Sectional Topographies" are even more generative; the projects in this section are experienced vertically as well as horizontally, move us from one space to the next, and extend their influence to frame our perception of the site. The theme "Program Effect" reveals the multiple programmatic influences in design. "Episodic Monumentality" describes the creation of a series of loosely related events, rendered in materials, color, shape, and light that become memorable. And the projects in "Additions Interventions" show how the existing structures bring immediate, palpable, and measurable context to the new designs. The categories are not mutually exclusive. Projects possess qualities that would make them at home in more than one chapter. No one category appears more important than the others. But they are helpful tools to understanding the work, dissecting what was important, how issues were examined, and how responses were made.

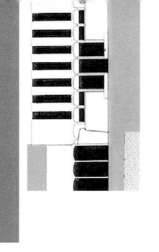

Architecture is most commonly thought of as "building," quite separate from the landscape that surrounds it. The concept of Building Landscape weaves the two together, to the extent where there may be no clear definition of where one ends and where the other begins. Demarcation between the building as it meets the ground, or as it defines space within the confines of its walls, is purposely fuzzy. Yet, we often find in these projects an extension of the building wall, which may reach out into the landscape, claiming green environs as architecture, as part of the realm in which design holds sway. In some cases it manifests itself as an articulation of the plane upon which the building sits, in others the architecture submerges beneath the ground, burrowing into the landscape.

Within this context, Building Landscape considers nature as a built condition, versus the untamed landscape of woodland or pasture. This landscape is far from primordial, but rather carefully considered and defined by the designer. Land forms are molded, leveled, or elevated in relation to the building itself. Spaces open and closed work together, creating a whole that is larger than just the building and the land it rests upon. The building and the landscape are equal partners.

Building Landscape offers an open, inclusive condition—one that invites addition. The relationship between building and land can be extended in ways the designers may not have contemplated. As such, building and landscape co-evolve over time, subject to interpretation by succeeding generations.

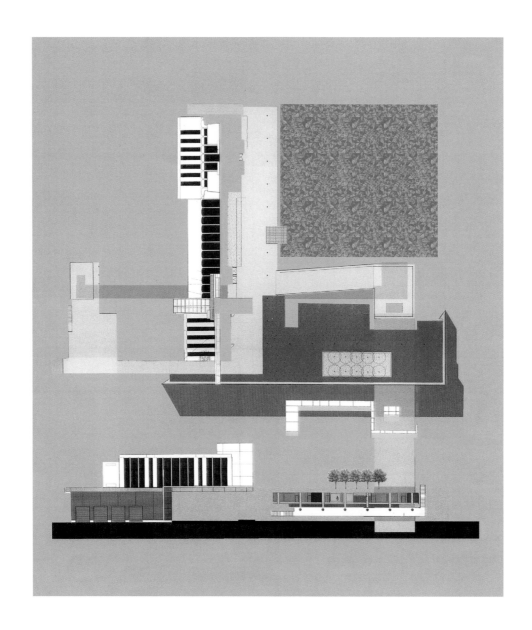

BARONE CAMPUS CENTER, FAIRFIELD UNIVERSITY
FAIRFIELD, CONNECTICUT

Fairfield University's existing campus center, built in the 1960s, is the literal and figurative heart of the campus. Occupying a geographic midpoint within the university, the campus center serves as the social crossroads of campus life, assimilating important student programs and activities. Clearly intended to sit as a pristine object within the landscape, the existing campus center awkwardly straddles the sloping site and adjacent parking lots.

The design of the addition recognizes the closed nature of the original building, which resists engagement or attachment. Instead of fracturing the center with what would no doubt result in a forced relationship, the architects took the opposite approach. The new Barone Campus Center is conceived as a plinth for the existing building, giving it a firm base. At the same time, the solution opens the site to include campus center activities beyond the confines of the original structure. This new complex houses the student lounge, student organizations, meeting rooms, central student mail facility, and service dock. In the second phase, the original 65,000-square-foot student center is to be renovated for expanded dining facilities. The building land-scape of the plinth lawn serves as a gathering space for daytime activities, while the plinth's transparent, luminous edge glows at night revealing the workings of students within. In a subtle shift, the new building in effect places the original building on a pedestal, yet moves the locus of action to the addition, which now contains the entrance to the entire campus center complex.

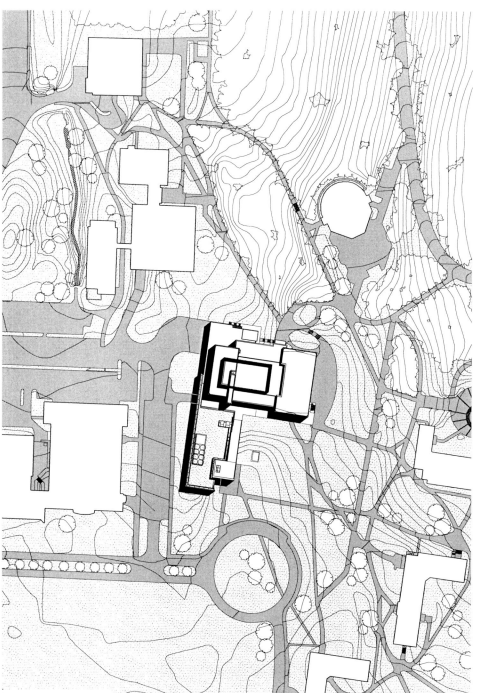

ABOVE   existing student center

LEFT   site plan

FACING PAGE   study model of plinth strategy

0   130 ft

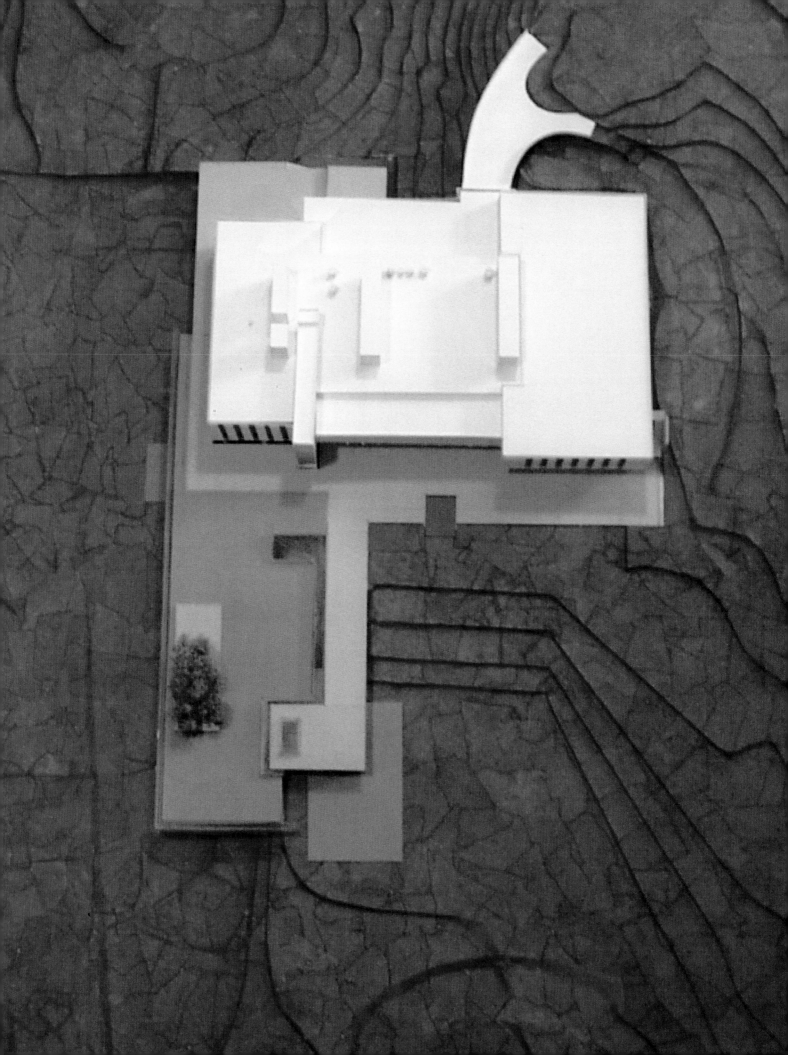

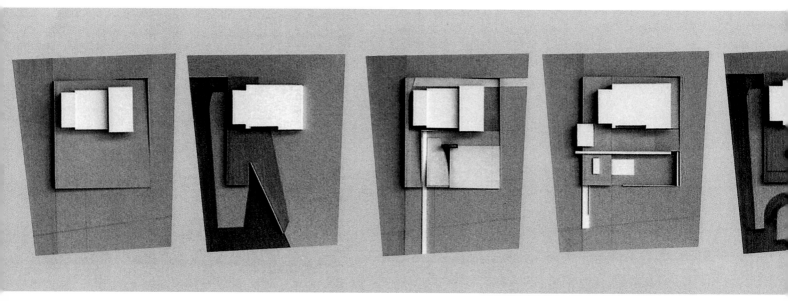

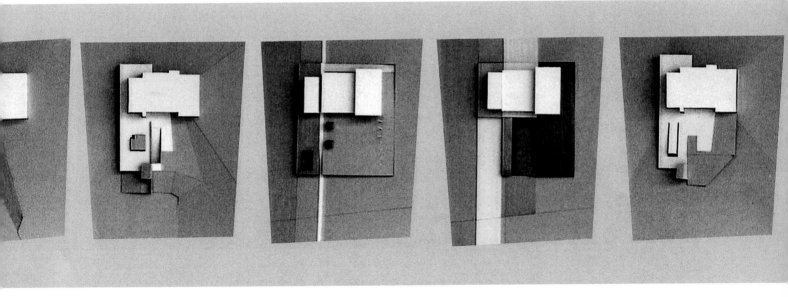

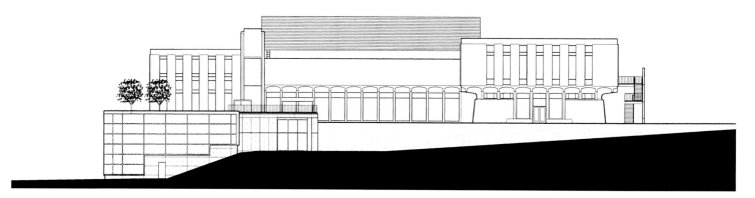

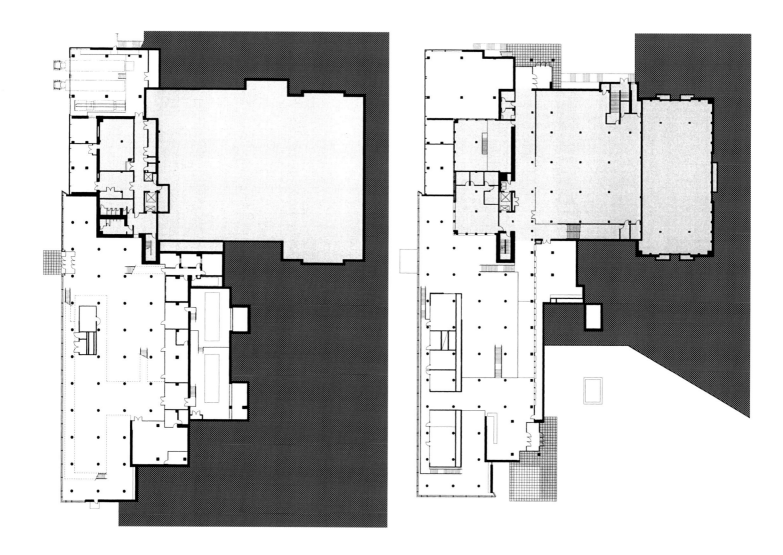

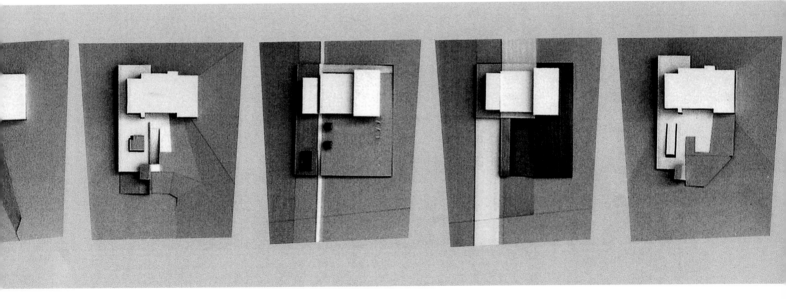

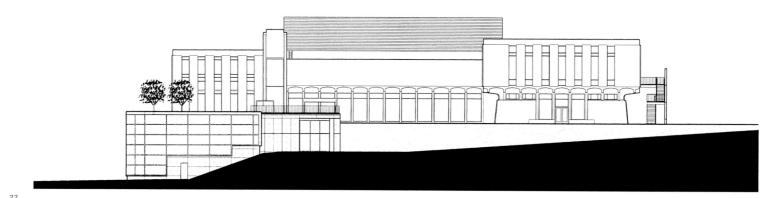

22

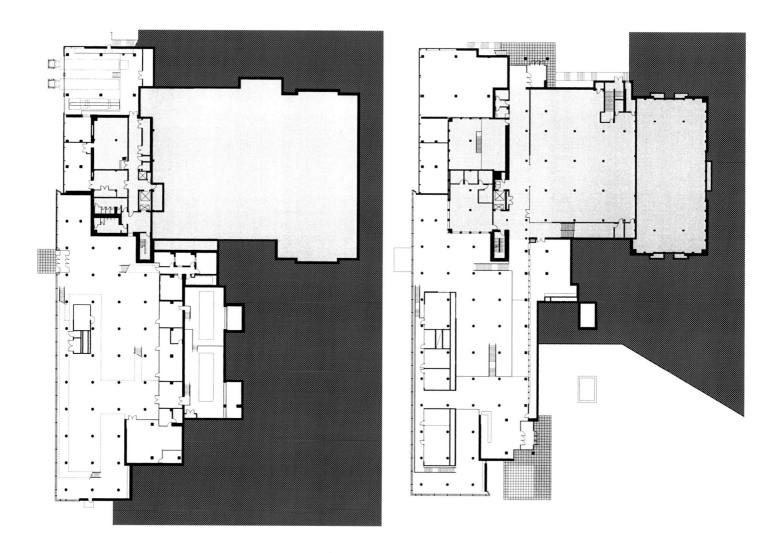

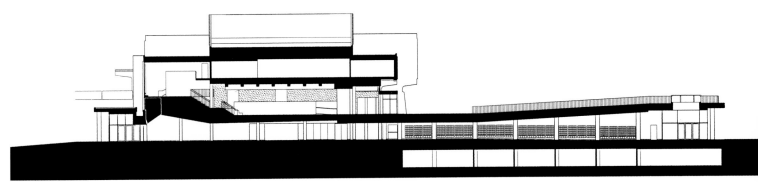

23

FACING PAGE TOP   north elevation

FACING PAGE LEFT   first floor plan with existing shaded

FACING PAGE RIGHT   second floor plan with existing shaded

TOP   longitudinal section

BOTTOM   existing building third floor plan and new roof plaza

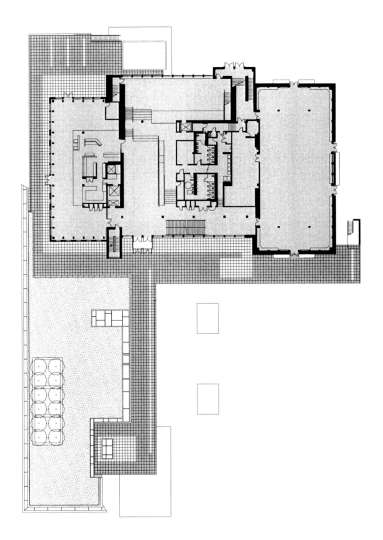

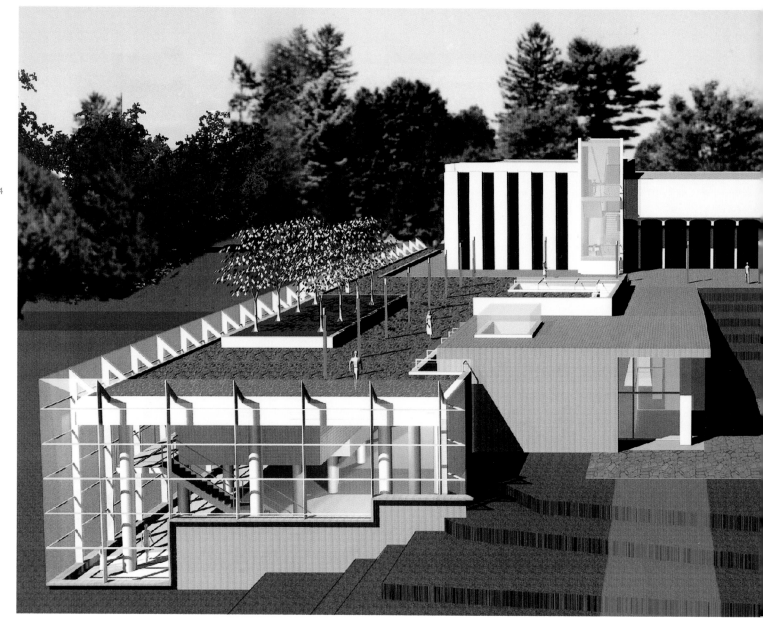

ABOVE   new building creates a base for the old

NEAR RIGHT   skylights allow glimpses of world above

FAR RIGHT   student lounge space

JOAN WEILL ADIRONDACK LIBRARY, PAUL SMITH'S COLLEGE
PAUL SMITH'S, NEW YORK

Situated in the heart of New York's Adirondack State Park, this library will provide state-of-the-art information technology services for the college and serve as the archive and resource center for the park. The building is linked to the rich heritage of Adirondack great camp architecture through the use of simple materials left to age naturally. Broadband and wireless information technologies are provided throughout the building. The technology is woven through to seamlessly support the users, and allow the primary expression and celebration to be the landscape beyond.

The building is sited along Lower Saint Regis Lake, on a generous open space that affords views of the lake and mountains beyond. Continuous with the landscape, it is organized as a linear structure running east-west, parallel to the lake edge. Its southern edge contains the general collections stacks and quiet study areas, affording light and dramatic views of the Adirondack range. The northern edge contains support and mechanical spaces and is covered over with earth berms to provide natural insulation. The site of the library had been cleared and flattened in the mid 19th century. The

library's design recreates the memory of the landscape before the hill was leveled, and makes the new contours part of the building's exploitation of light and views to the south and an earth's blanket protecting it from its northern exposure. The library is a full story below grade on the north side. In approaching the building, one sees a more diminutive structure, which belies its size of nearly 45,000 square feet. The bulk of the building is further reduced by rotating certain plan components and giving these components unique identifying roof forms.

30

ABOVE   view toward Saint Regis Mountain

RIGHT   environmental design strategies

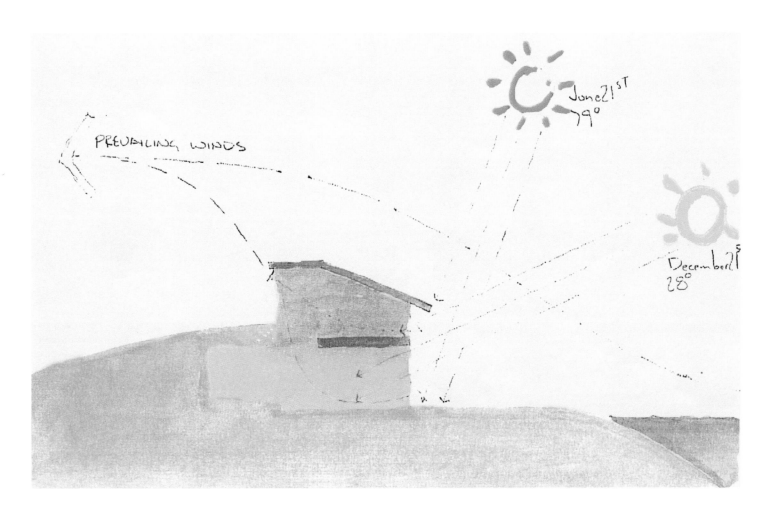

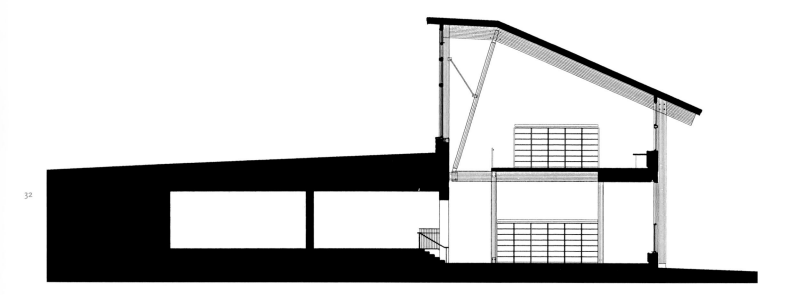

32

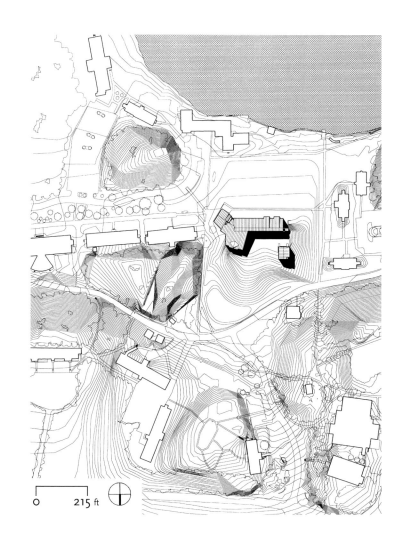

0 215 ft

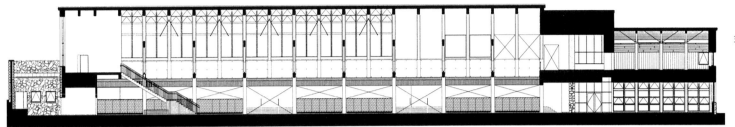

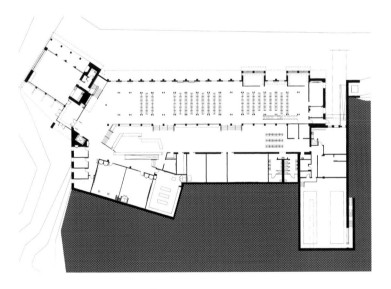

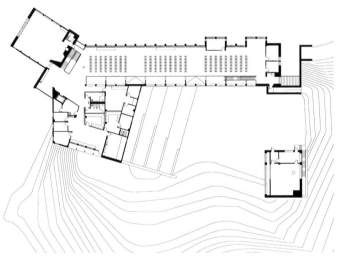

FACING PAGE TOP   transverse section

FACING PAGE BOTTOM   site plan

TOP   longitudinal section through general collections

BOTTOM LEFT   ground floor plan

BOTTOM RIGHT   upper level plan

FAR LEFT library with Adirondack Room in foreground

LEFT model showing library roof contour

RIGHT top floor offers dramatic space

FAR RIGHT overhangs protect windows from solar gain

WAIDNER LIBRARY, DICKINSON COLLEGE
CARLISLE, PENNSYLVANIA

The Waidner Library addition at Dickinson College is a radical departure from the existing Spahr Library in consideration of the architecture and landscape of the older campus. The existing 1960s library was out of character with most of the campus. The new building weaves modern and historic elements to form a new whole reintegrating the original library into the campus. The 46,000-square-foot addition links into the existing library on the west side with a glazed connection that clearly separates old from new. However, these glassy walls replicate the older library's tripartite horizontal window division—a subtle, harmonic reference. In plan, the addition is the same width as Spahr, establishing a clear relationship to the existing building and the broader campus organization. It is as if a section of the older library has been sliced off and pulled away, and the void infilled with a glazed connector. The connector wall steps back on the south side to allow room for an old Sycamore tree. On the north side of the connector, a new terraced garden connects to Dickinson Walk, a pedestrian way that links the building to dorms and the student union.

Waidner reflects the materials of the older campus buildings, some of which date from the Civil War. The oval reading room to the north, a slightly canted wall into which are set group study spaces, a thick battered stone wall lined with window seats, a two-story bay window housing lounge space, and the gracefully curved glazed connector wall all serve to reach out to the existing landscape and to tie into it and the well-used pedestrian routes. The transparency of the new building is welcoming, revealing activity within. Its monumental entry canopy is scaled to join new and old buildings.

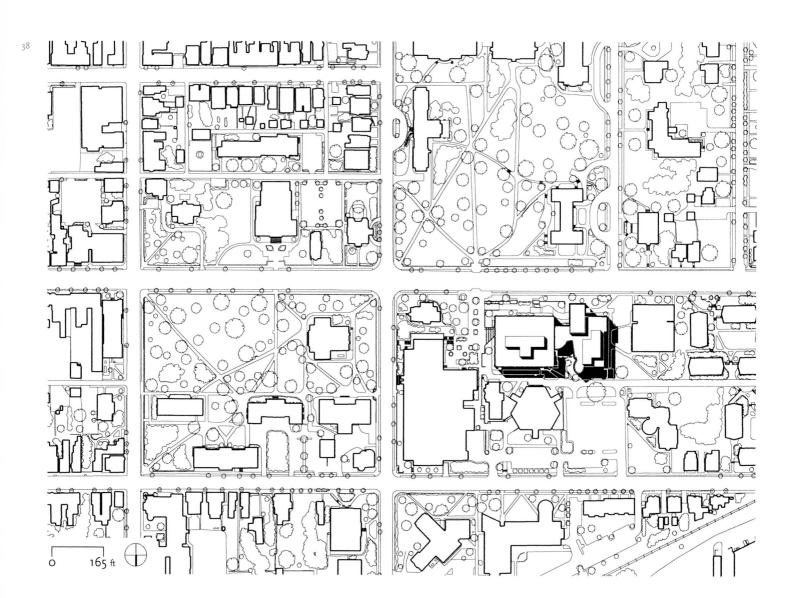

38

165 ft

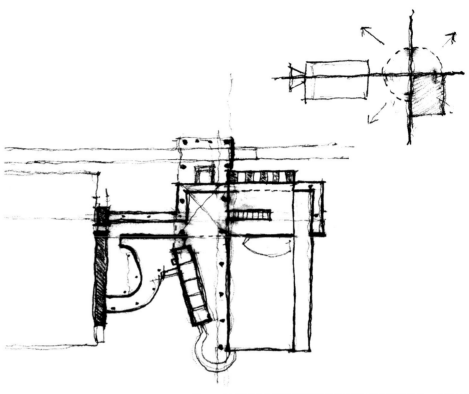

LEFT   campus plan

ABOVE RIGHT   connections to existing building and context

BELOW RIGHT   organizational study

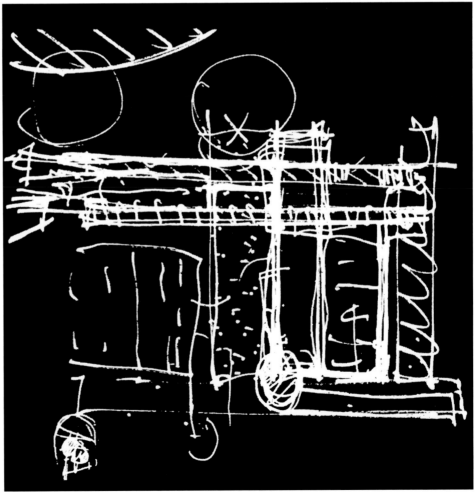

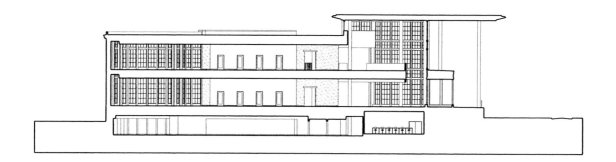

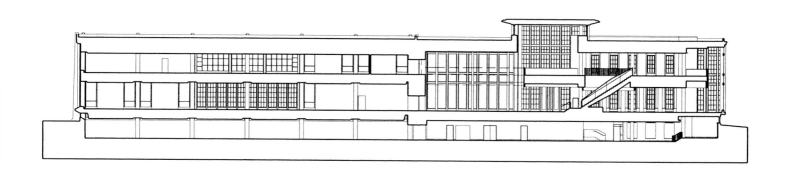

FACING PAGE TOP   transverse section through addition

FACING PAGE BOTTOM   longitudinal section through
existing and new

BELOW   first floor plan with existing shaded

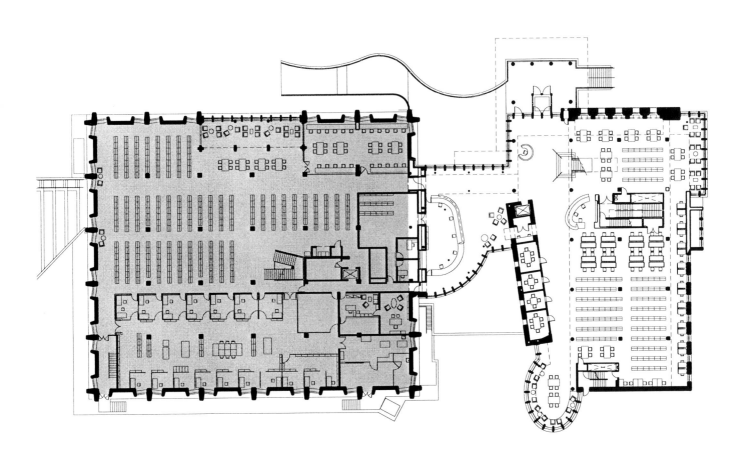

ABOVE   private study spaces abound

NEAR RIGHT   window seat provides a quiet corner

CENTER RIGHT   natural materials relate to context

FAR RIGHT   double-height reading space

EXTREME RIGHT   light and views are abundant

45

COLLEGE CAMPUS, FRANKLIN W. OLIN COLLEGE OF ENGINEERING
NEEDHAM, MASSACHUSETTS

The mission of the new Franklin W. Olin College of Engineering is to create "entrepreneurial engineers"; engineers engaged in broad cultural needs and interests. The new campus explores the formal interaction of building and landscape on a large scale. The campus is conceived of as both inwardly focused and expansive. Abutting an existing college campus, the elliptical central green conceptually, formally, and spatially anchors the design.

The site slopes from west to east, falling 60 feet before rising to an opposing wooded hillside. The long axis of the oval is parallel to the site contours, establishing the approach to the campus and encompassing the broad eastern vista. A system of brick terraces and walls negotiates and registers the changes in grade, as well as provides level "platforms" for each building. The oval is set one floor below the high point of the site. This sectional offset allows a series of programmatic relationships concealing support spaces uphill and opening public spaces to the views downhill. Small-scale inflections of the oval ground the grand gesture in the local setting. Within and around the oval, spaces are created that invite students to stop, lounge, and inhabit it as a central community space, while providing glimpses of spaces and vistas beyond the oval.

A monumental colonnade, part of the main lab building and student center, forms three-quarters of the oval. The remaining southeast quadrant opens to the landscape and contains the library/administration building and a future lab building. From within the oval, the colonnade serves as a visual frame for the other buildings. The edge of the housing complex, along with the future lab building, forms a cascading lawn directed at the opposing hillside.

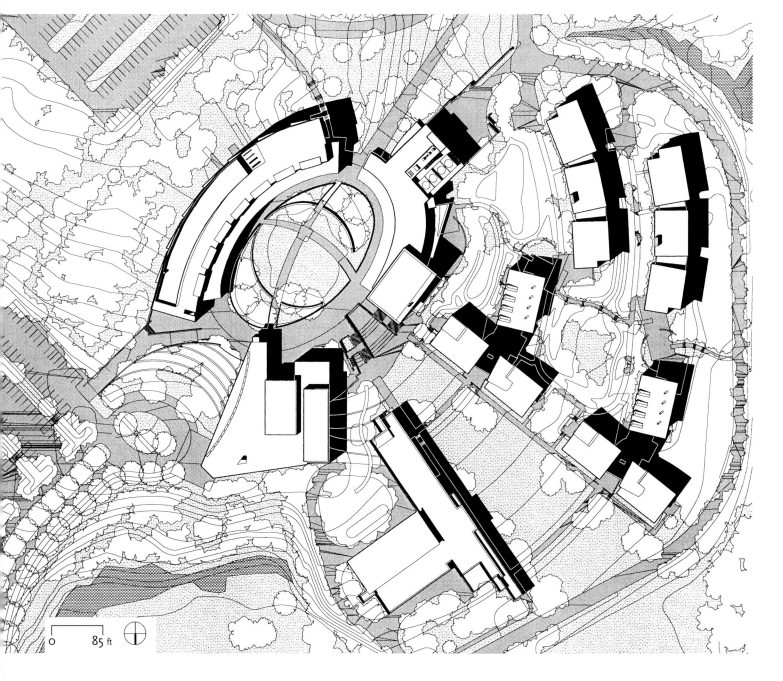

0 ⊢ 85 ft ⊕

FACING PAGE   campus plan

ABOVE   campus models

FOLLOWING PAGES   study models and site section

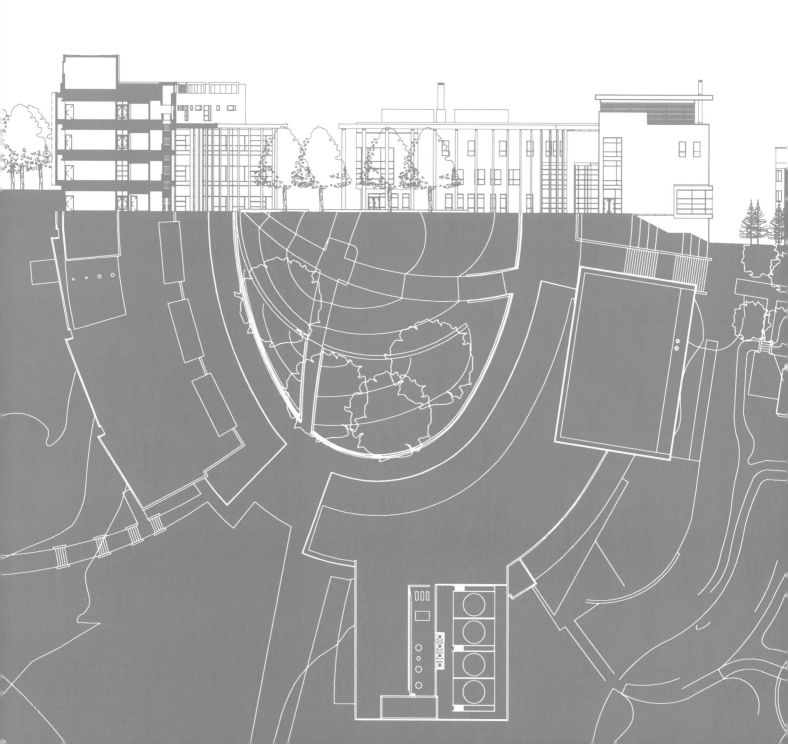

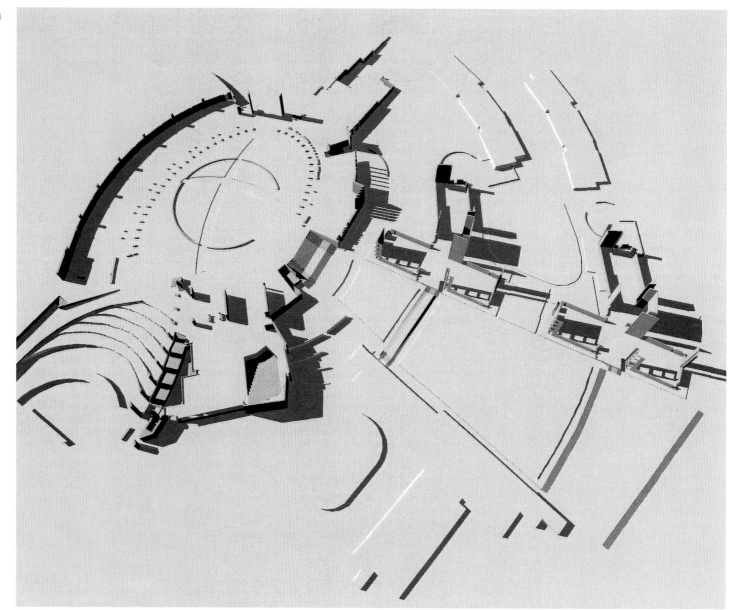

FACING PAGE   illustration of topographic organization

TOP   library and administration building

BOTTOM   laboratory/classroom building from campus entry

TOP   view toward student center

BOTTOM   view toward residence halls

FACING PAGE TOP   library and administration building from
student center colonnade

FACING PAGE BOTTOM   laboratory building from library and
administration building

56

FRANKLIN W. OLIN COLLEGE OF ENGINEERING

RELATIVE OBJECTS

The architecture of the American college campus often suggests the form of new buildings that might be added to it. One approach to collegiate building design is to heed the call for an implicit order that the existing campus makes, and to design accordingly. In this way, some campus buildings are conceived as Relative Objects—placed within a context of the campus, they speak the same language of the architecture that is already there and, in a manner of speaking, "complete" the sentence.

Design that responds to Relative Objects takes the measure of the buildings that are already there, and expands on existing systems. It is attentive to classic campus planning, often distinguished by axial arrangements, clearly defined open spaces, and restrained form-making. In most cases, the new building's most important urban function is to play a supporting role in helping to define the larger idea of the campus plan. Rather than idiosyncratic, unilaterally-sculptural buildings, those designed as Relative Objects seek to find a place within the family of spaces and forms that are connected to each other throughout the campus and that may give the institution its sense of place.

Ultimately, this approach to architecture accepts a given order. It seeks to enhance it, strengthen it, make it more complete. It may be inventive in its interpretation of that order. It may make the users of the buildings and spaces more aware of a pre-existing condition. In some cases, the addition of the new building may bring a campus's latent spatial system to closure, completing the idea of another designer from an earlier generation.

63

JOHN DEAVER DRINKO LIBRARY, MARSHALL UNIVERSITY
HUNTINGTON, WEST VIRGINIA

Drinko Library is located just south of Old Main, the most venerable building on Marshall University's campus. Old Main has the look of a castle, with its sturdy red brick walls, rusticated stone base and banding, and a central tower with four crenulated turrets. The university wanted the library to relate to this campus landmark. Drinko has substantial walls of red brick with a light stone banding. On its west facade two solid shafts rise to suggest the towers of Old Main.

Red brick facades extend south and north, bending around with a graceful curve to stop abruptly at a large, five-story glass cylinder—the building's tallest element. This linchpin of activity, through which one can see the motion along several staircases and a reading room, marks Drinko's main entrance, where the library's "old" and "new" personalities merge. To the south of this cylinder, a contemporary facade of glass and stucco appears, behind which is a welcoming café on the first floor, and a reading room and administrative offices above. A stainless steel canopy arcs along a pedestrian path and connects back into the entry cylinder with a wavy tongue that passes through the glass walls and hovers over the circulation desk.

Inside, Drinko's spaces are arranged with a logic that places people near windows and open vistas, while the collection and computer spaces reside at the building's heart. The glassy rotunda serves as an important orienting device in this large building, with stairways clinging to or flying through it.

64

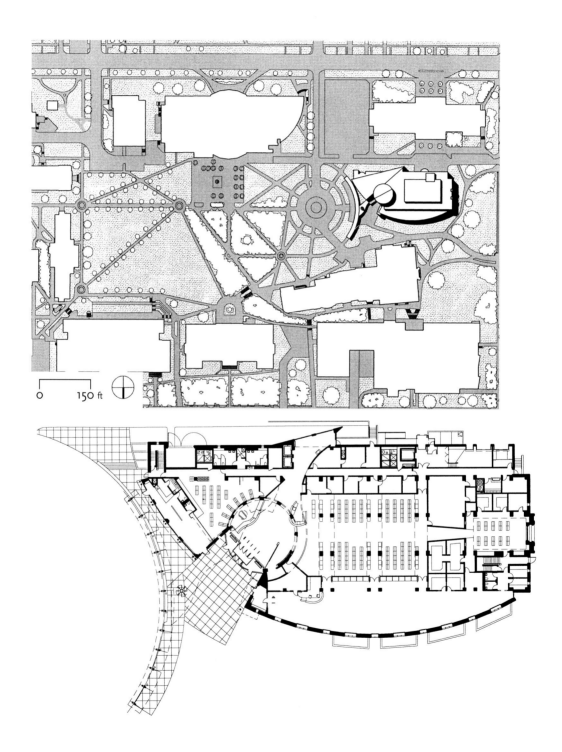

0   150 ft

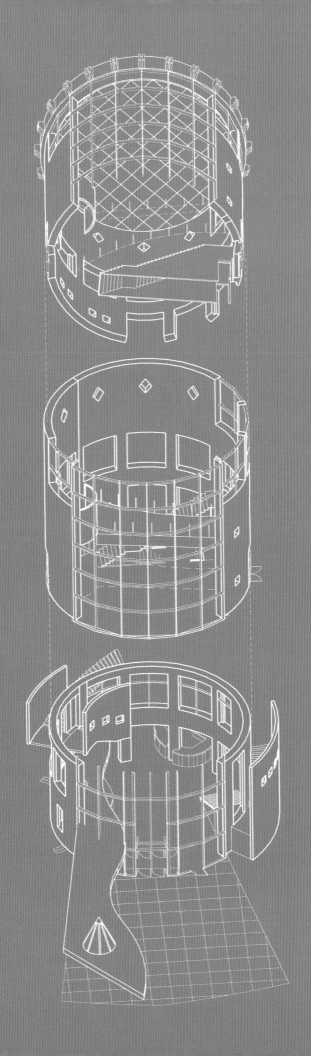

66

FACING PAGE   upper atrium

TOP LEFT   main entry

TOP RIGHT   circulation desk

BOTTOM LEFT   curves define pathways

BOTTOM CENTER   main lobby reference desk

BOTTOM RIGHT   bridge in upper atrium

KOLENBRANDER-HARTER INFORMATION CENTER, MOUNT UNION COLLEGE
ALLIANCE, OHIO

The Information Center occupies a key location on the east side of campus and encourages pedestrian traffic to the inner campus through its generous central lobby. In fact, the building is strategically placed on long north-south, east-west axes in relation to existing campus buildings and pedestrian routes so that it creates a gateway. By doing so, it reinforces other axially-arranged buildings on campus.

The Information Center contains a broad collection of program uses. Ten classrooms/ computer laboratories, two multi-media laboratories, an academic wing of 21 faculty offices, 300 reader seats, the Computer Science Department, Library staff offices, a faculty lounge, shelving for 135,000 volumes, and a coffee shop are housed in a 65,000-square-foot addition. Like a series of houses along an interior street, the library, teaching wing, faculty offices, and 24-hour reading room are all entered from the cross-axial lobby. The new space is connected seamlessly to the original library of 45,000 square feet, with the main entrance relocated to an at-grade location in the new structure to provide full accessibility.

The Information Center meets the sky in a way that recalls the composition and layering of a prominent existing building. From the west, its gently curved barrel roof appears to be a thin-edged lid. Seen from the north, the glazing of the reading room emphasizes this curve as it meets the roof, forming an identity as it meets the sky. From the east the roof disappears behind a facade of buff-colored brick, which is pulled forward at an angle, referring to the pond across the road.

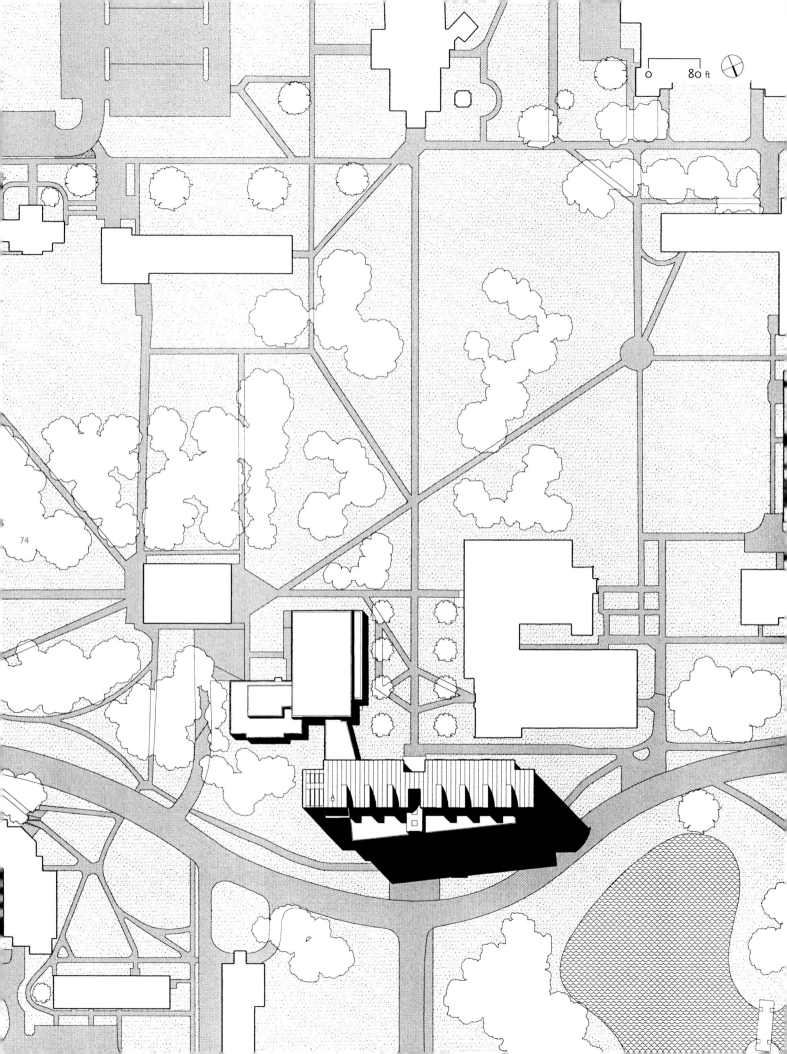

74

FACING PAGE   site plan illustrating axial alignment with chapel

TOP   third floor plan with existing shaded

BOTTOM   first floor plan with existing shaded

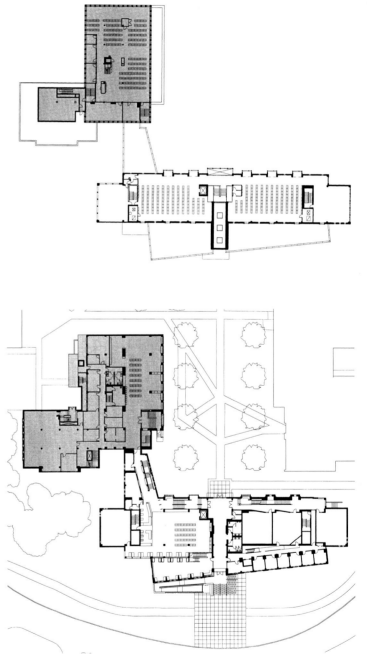

76

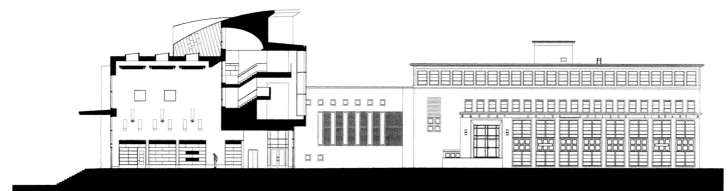

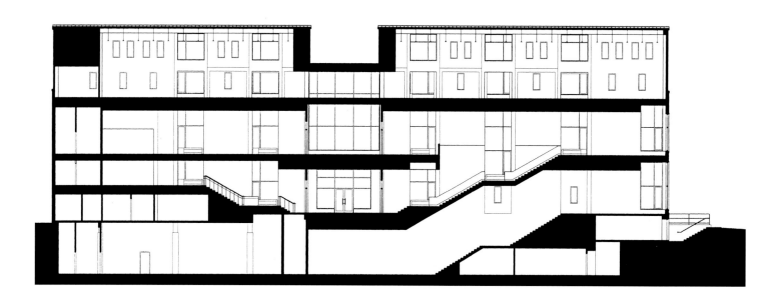

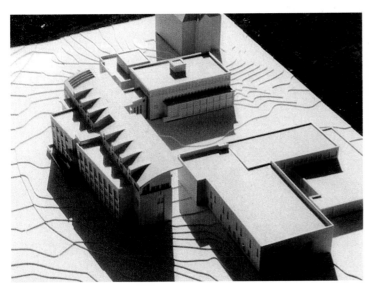

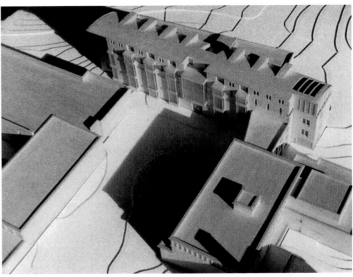

FACING PAGE   main lobby

TOP   window seats line circulation routes

BOTTOM   third floor north reading room

MORGAN LIBRARY, COLORADO STATE UNIVERSITY
FORT COLLINS, COLORADO

The challenge of the addition at Morgan Library was to redress the deficiencies of an L-shaped library, which created pockets of dead space and thwarted clear circulation. The program required 109,000 additional square feet of stacks and reader space, and the university's president asked for "an elegant solution" and a landmark, located at the southern end of a central campus plaza.

The solution took the form of two additions, which begin with a new entrance in the plaza, behind a new curved entry wall. The wall, scaled to the plaza, is curved just enough to capture the sun, and is made from locally-quarried red sandstone. The light shimmers across the rough texture of the rock most intensely at first light of dawn and again at sunset. Once inside, one can move through the space to the enclosed reading garden, or follow the plan shift to the west, moving through the longer leg of the original building to the second addition's sweeping wall of glass facing the Front Range of the Rocky Mountains. The plan that emerged, with the additions in place, corrects the original library's L-shaped plan and ensures flexibility of furniture and collections arrangements.

The university wanted a library that would provide a focal point for the campus. Morgan now serves that role. Proving the success of the building, students regularly stand for their graduation pictures in front of its curved entry wall—a backdrop that immediately identifies their alma mater.

DESIGN ARCHITECT: PERRY DEAN ROGERS | PARTNERS ARCHITECTS
ASSOCIATED ARCHITECT: LUIS O. ACOSTA ARCHITECTS OF DENVER

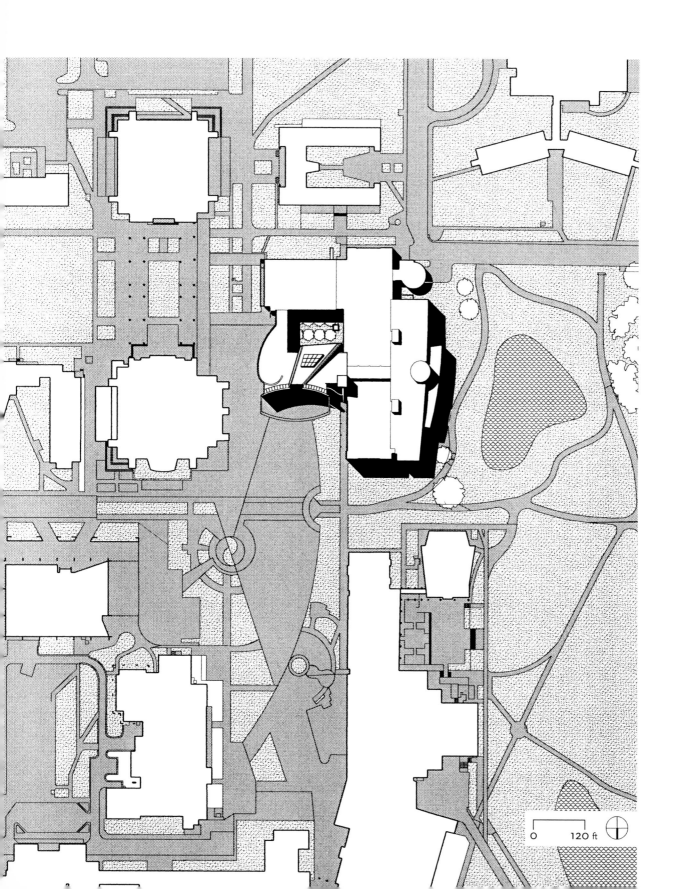

0   120 ft

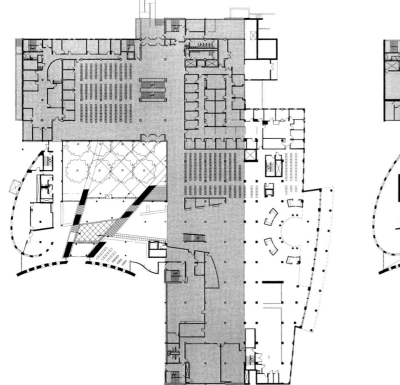

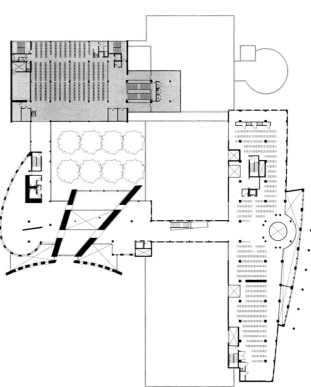

86   TOP   glassy elevation looking toward Rocky Mountains

MIDDLE   main entry plaza

BOTTOM   courtyard

FACING PAGE   Colorado's sun creates strong patterns of light and shadow

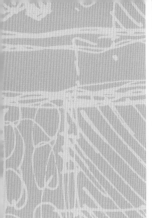

Architecture can reveal to us and accentuate the experience of moving from one place to another. The context of Sectional Topographies relates to how the building's volume moves us as we make our way from one space to the next, experiencing the architecture vertically and horizontally. Ascent and descent are magnified, and the design makes us more aware of our bodies rising and falling in space.

Movement inside the buildings is revealed through its sectional experience—seeing people throughout the structure engaged with it on various levels. One perceives how the building moves across the site, particularly in cases where there are dramatic changes in grade. This can be experienced within the building, as spaces move up or down, or by moving around the outside of a series of buildings that take their place at different levels as they are positioned on the site.

Sectional Topography can also be read in a single direction. For example, the building may offer a wealth of spatial experiences as one moves east-west, while in the north-south direction the range of spaces read and perceived in section may be limited. Program, site configuration, and adjacent structures can all have a determining influence.

UPPER SCHOOL, SHADY HILL SCHOOL
CAMBRIDGE, MASSACHUSETTS

Built in the late 1920s, the Shady Hill campus and its buildings reflect the pedagogical philosophy of the school. Single-story, two-classroom buildings, each housing and identified with a single grade, are arranged in a compact plan that fosters informal interaction and a close academic community. Each classroom consists of the main teaching space, a group study room, and a teacher's office. In addition to windows, many of these spaces are distinguished with uniquely configured light monitors. Narrow pathways and porches provide transition points from one building to another.

The new project consists of three new classroom buildings, a renovated building, and a refined landscape design. The project constraints included a tight site and an architectural language of small-scale, wood-frame, gray-painted buildings with double-hung windows that the client wished to preserve. Analysis of the existing campus plan suggested an organization akin to the board game "Chutes and Ladders." Straight east-west "ladders" extend from campus end to end, threading three precincts: upper and lower schools, with administration and library facilities in the middle. Irregular north-south "chutes" traverse the sloped topography. The new design seeks to accentuate this organization, making one aware of the intimate community spaces as one moves between them and from precinct to precinct. Upper and lower schools are marked with courtyard gathering spaces linked together by a central green with a flagpole. Abundant natural light is brought in through the sculptural roof monitors that also give each classroom a unique ceiling configuration. Outside, the monitors provide each building with its individual character, and collectively suggest a landscape of forms.

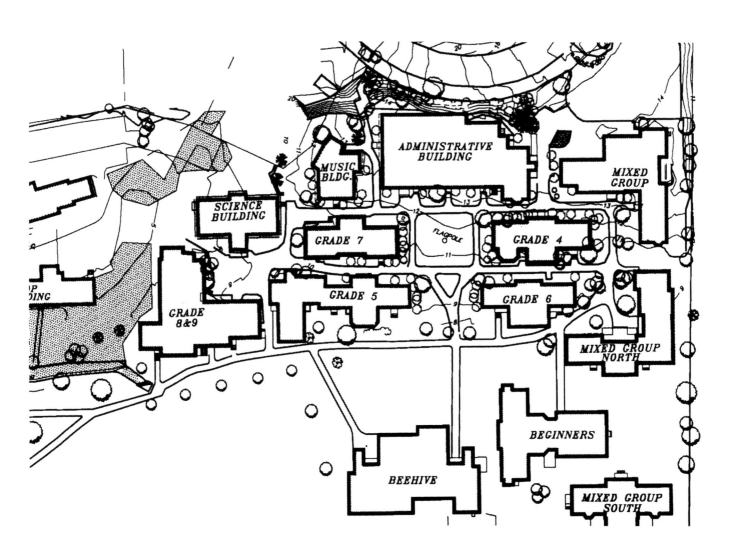

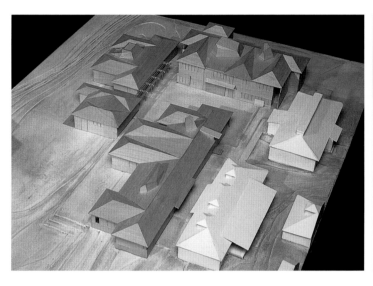

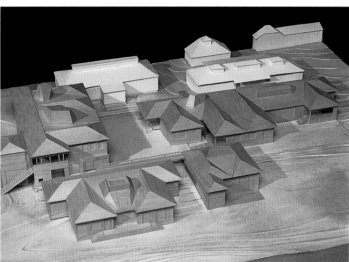

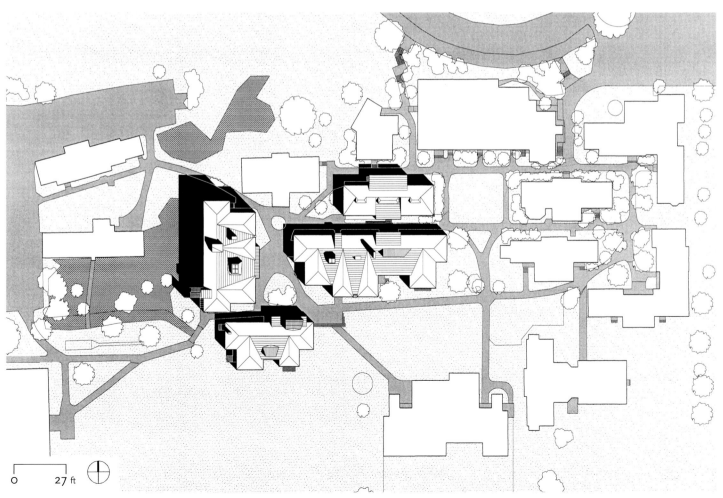

O   27 ft

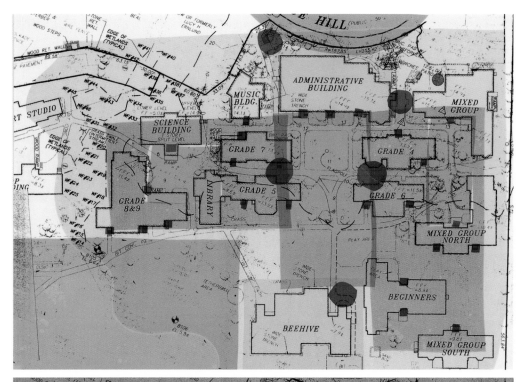

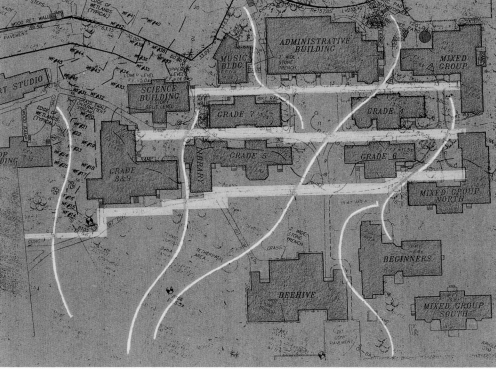

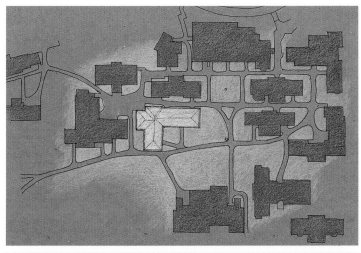

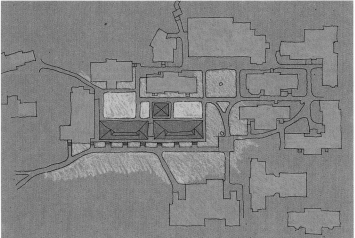

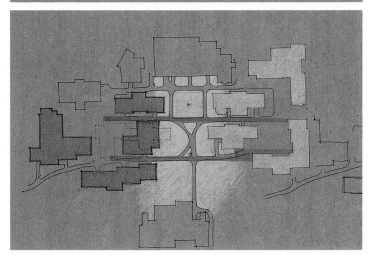

BELOW   floor plans

FACING PAGE TOP   south elevations

FACING PAGE UPPER MIDDLE   longitudinal site section

FACING PAGE LOWER MIDDLE   transverse site section

FACING PAGE BOTTOM   selected light monitor details

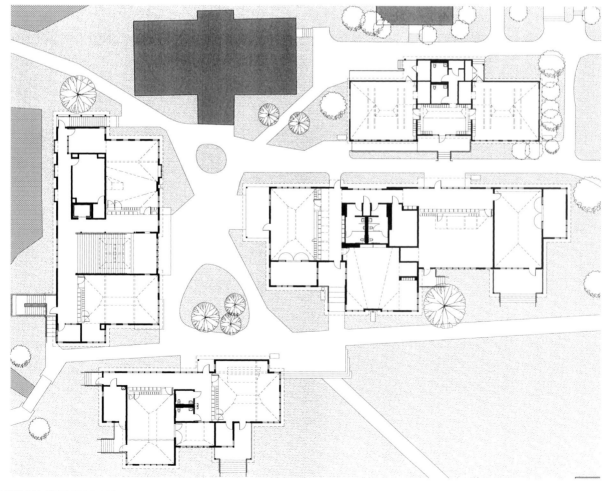

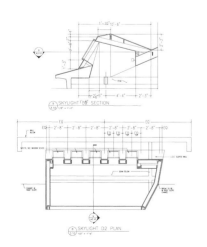

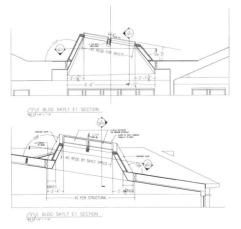

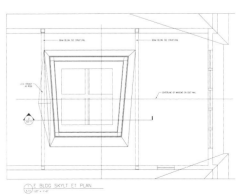

RIGHT AND FACING PAGE   unique ways of introducing
daylight make every room singular
FOLLOWING PAGES   views of exterior details and roofscapes

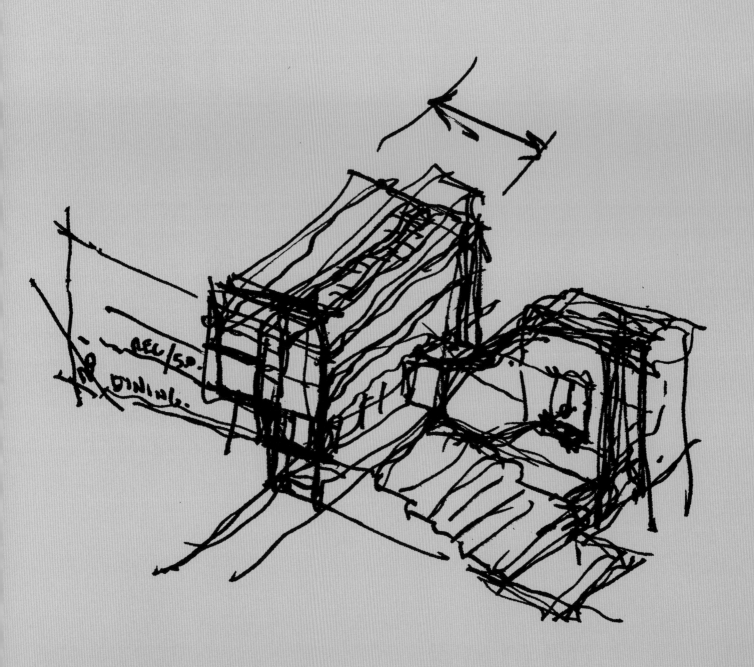

THE COMMONS, UNIVERSITY OF MARYLAND, BALTIMORE COUNTY
BALTIMORE, MARYLAND

The Commons is intentionally sited to shape a new campus formal lawn and to reinforce an existing campus informal quadrangle, bridging a 22-foot change in grade between these two important campus spaces. The "bridge" between these two spaces is the Commons, a 150,000-square-foot campus center located at the very heart of the campus that includes retail spaces, lounges, and food services along its length and major entrances at both ends. The building is site specific, following the topography as it rolls down from north to south, creating outdoor spaces that recognize pre-existing axes on the campus.

The Commons is designed as a "hill-town main street." Multiple levels provide a sense of theater and invite exploration. The multitude of opportunities on different levels to "see and be seen" enhances the visibility of the major spaces, and reinforces the building's sectional nature. For example, the Student Bazaar is a double-height space that offers vantages of other students moving around the building, and moving up and down the site. This space can also be viewed from the Recreational Multipurpose Room. This gives the building the "intensity of an ant hill," and it also accentuates the dramatic change of grade as it is expressed outside in a series of terraced green areas. These green areas offer welcome community spaces of different scales, and are located to take full advantage of the generous southern exposure.

DESIGN ARCHITECT: PERRY DEAN ROGERS | PARTNERS ARCHITECTS
ASSOCIATED ARCHITECT: DESIGN COLLECTIVE, INC. OF BALTIMORE

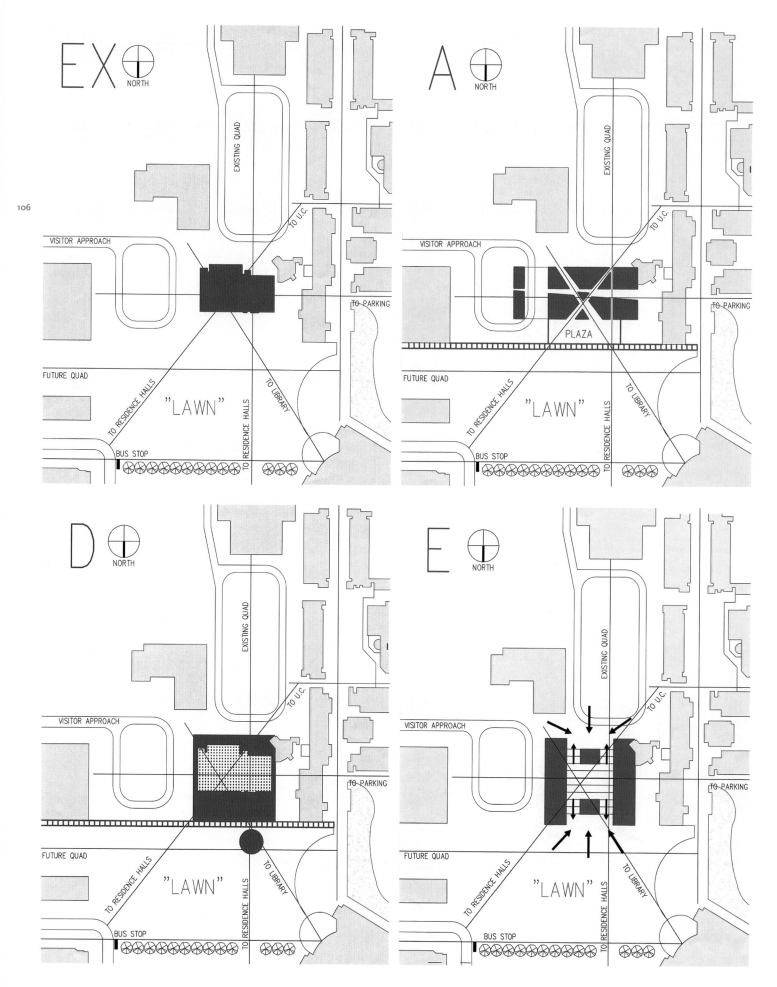

SECTIONAL TOPOGRAPHIES

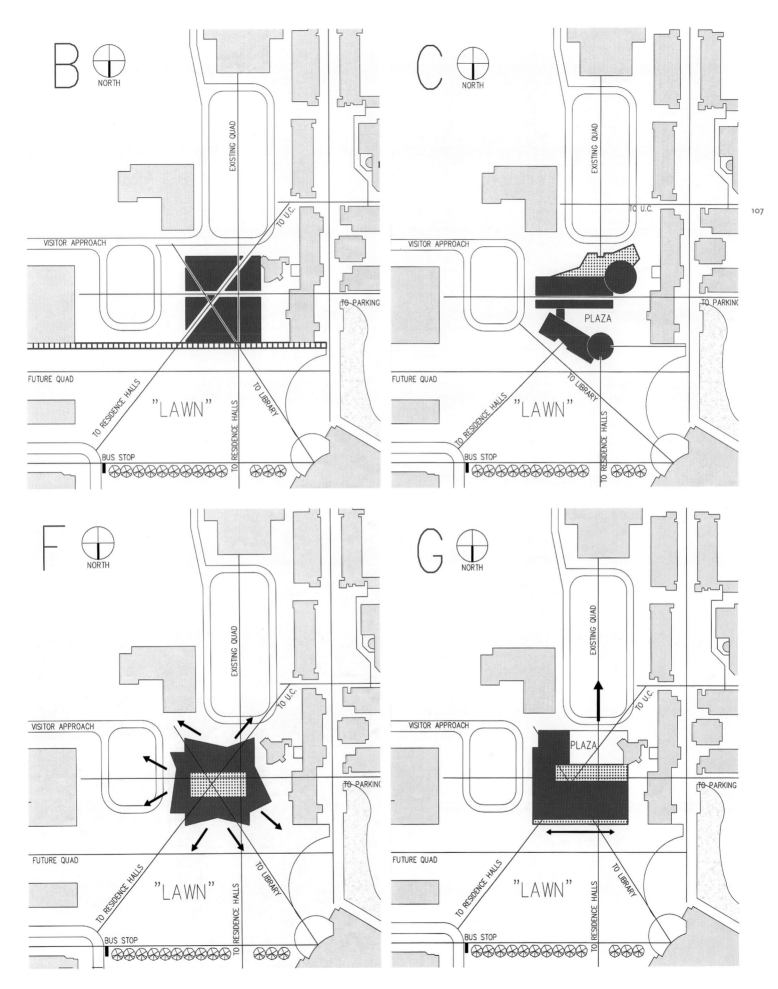

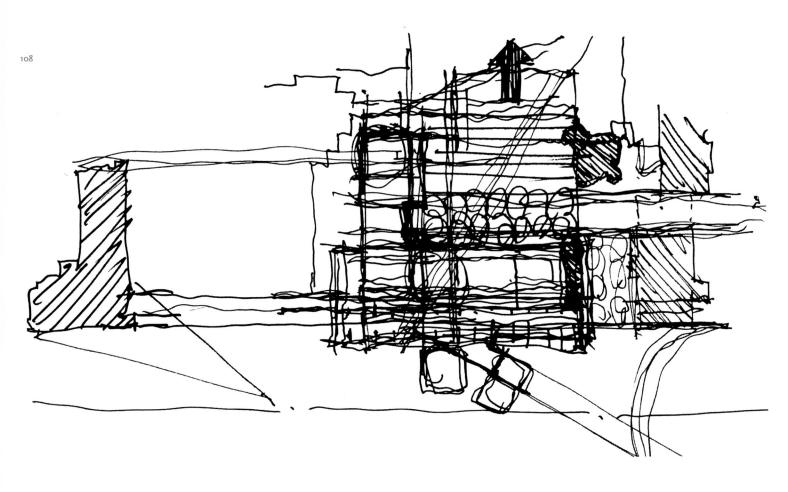

PREVIOUS PAGES   existing conditions and site planning
alternatives A-G

ABOVE   study model of building/site relationship

FACING PAGE   model studying building negotiating site

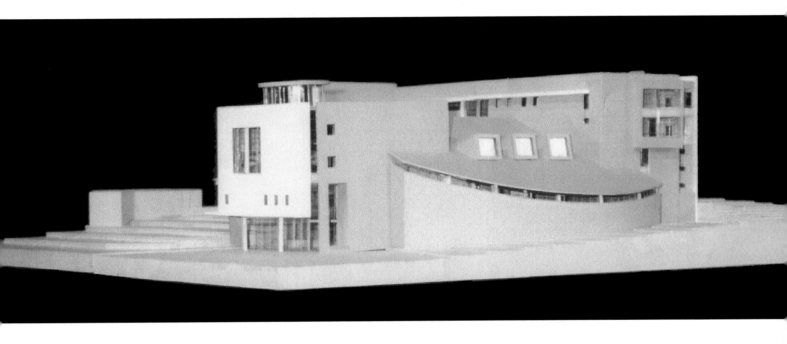

0   130 ft

LEFT   site plan

FACING PAGE TOP   second floor plan

FACING PAGE BOTTOM   first floor plan

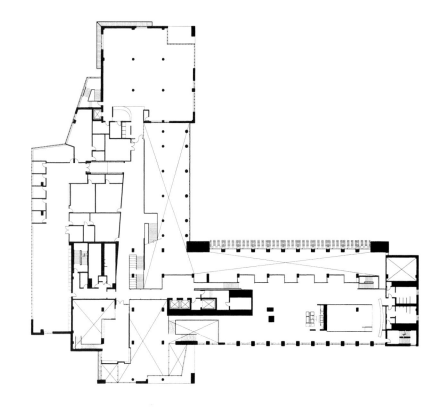

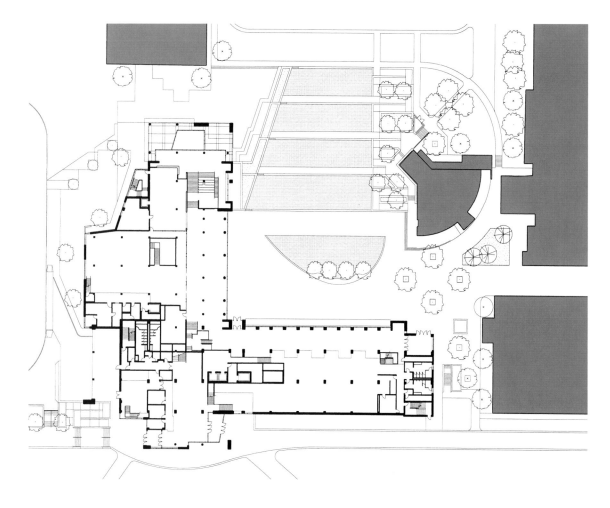

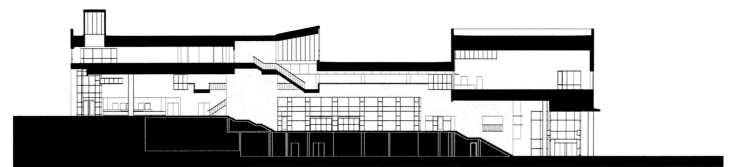

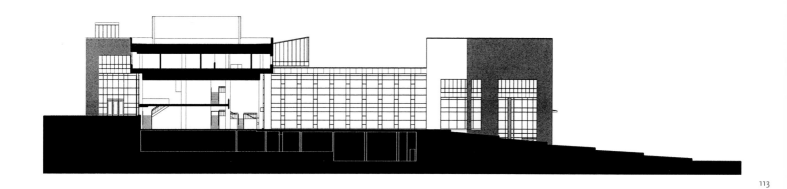

113

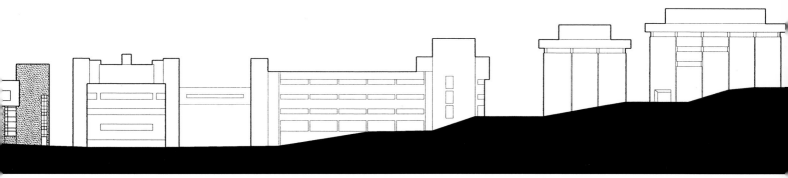

TOP LEFT   section through student bazaar

TOP RIGHT   section through dining hall and terraced lawn

BOTTOM   site section

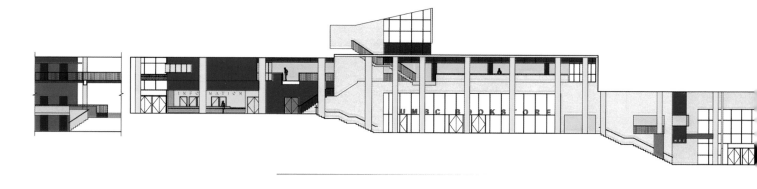

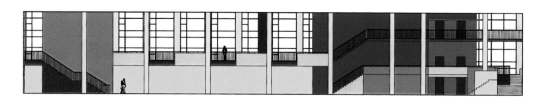

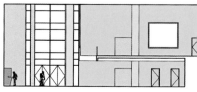

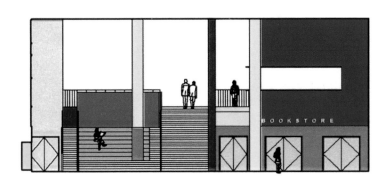

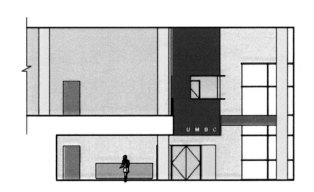

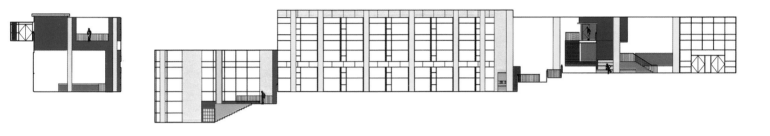

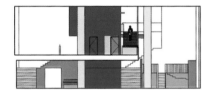

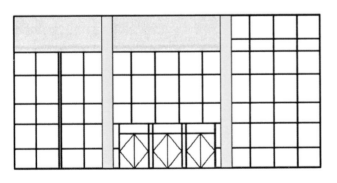
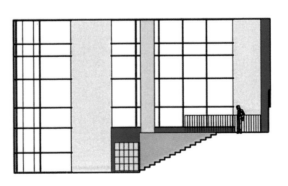

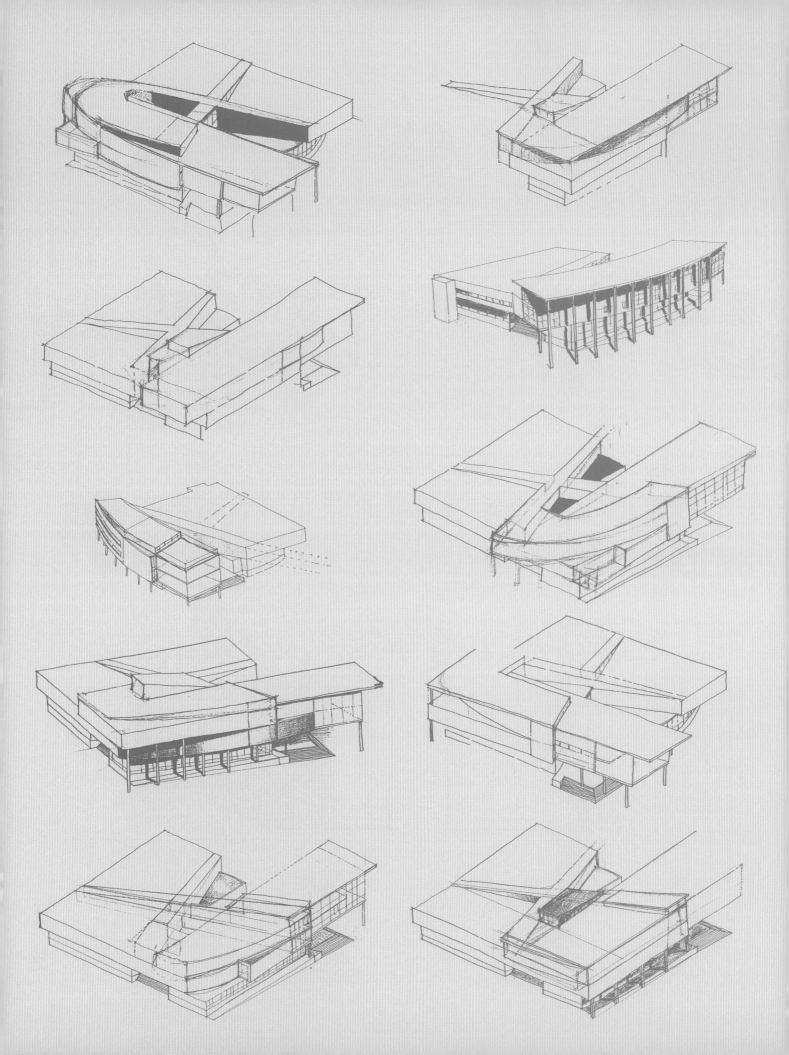

LIBRARY, ECKERD COLLEGE
ST. PETERSBURG, FLORIDA

Located east of the existing Cobb Library on the St. Petersburg, Florida campus, the new library will serve to increase the volume count and administrative requirements of Eckerd, and will connect to the Cobb at a single point, allowing both buildings to work together to serve the needs of the campus.

The new building has been shaped by embracing multiple prevailing site and programmatic forces. Lifting the entire building above grade, due to coastal water table levels, allows for a raised courtyard enhanced by the Florida climate. The primary book collection stacks and circulation department are located in a three-story bar to the north of this court. To the south is a two-story administration block behind a more public, double-height reading room facing directly onto the courtyard. North and south are connected by a glassy lobby, which allows for easily-monitored entry from the road to the east and the campus to the west. An intermediate level at the reading room houses the café, conveniently situated at the connection point from building to building. A bridge at this level connects directly into the mezzanine level of the Cobb Library.

The organization of the library on either side of an active courtyard, together with multiple-height spaces which transform fluidly into "book" and "office" zones, allow for ease of orientation for new and frequent visitors alike. Movement through the building has been prioritized to make one feel comfortable with constant visual orientation. The library allows for both outward views to the campus and Cobb Library, but also for an inward focus. The myriad activities of the rest of the building are generally perceivable from almost anywhere, but with necessary opportunity for quiet and calm.

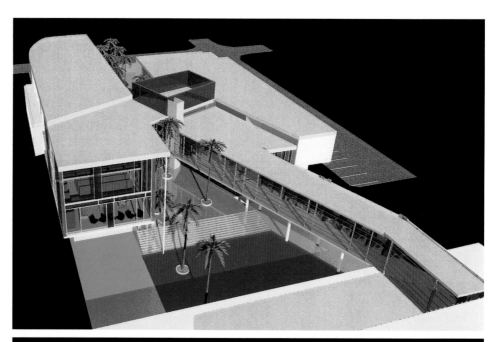

TOP   roof plan

MIDDLE   second and third floor plan

BOTTOM   first floor plan

FACING PAGE   site plan

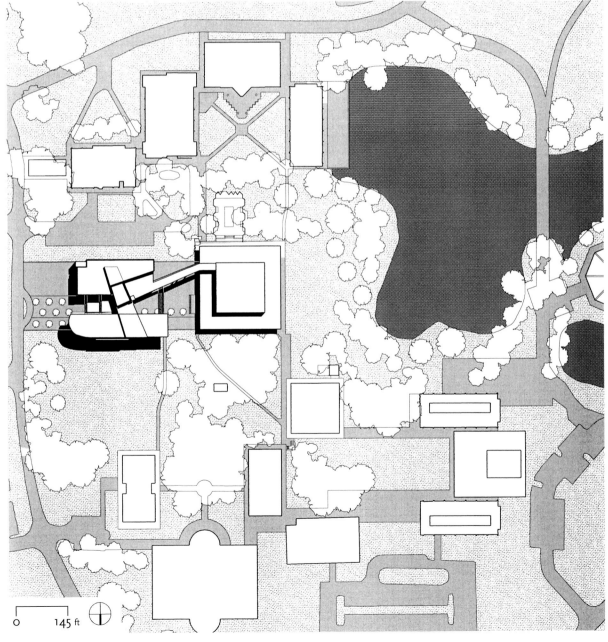

0 145 ft

PREVIOUS PAGES LEFT   entry from east

PREVIOUS PAGES TOP   entry from west

PREVIOUS PAGES MIDDLE   view to information commons

from library stacks

PREVIOUS PAGES BOTTOM   view to existing library from new

reading room

BEOW   south elevation diagram

PROGRAM EFFECT

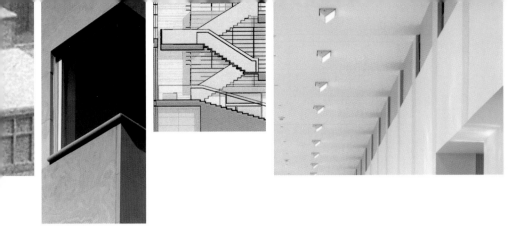

Context is reconsidered in light of the program. The boundary condition between programmatic accommodation and contextual resolution is brought into focus. Unlike the old dictum "Form Follows Function," the building program is construed to be specific to a place without compromising its irreducible components. The design of these buildings is driven from within. The distribution of the plan, the shape of the spaces, their location on a site, and the materials used may all be dictated by the client's programmatic needs.

This architecture utilizes the functional requirements as a well of inspiration for the design. Understanding the process inherent in the program is part of the architect's role. Within these constraints are often found the seeds of creativity, the starting point from which the building's design takes flight. Sometimes the design takes a tack inspired by a new interpretation of the client's needs that had not been previously considered. There are also instances where the architect helps rewrite the program to allow the building to yield greater amenities for the client and the users.

While Program Effect emphasizes how architecture is shaped from within, external influences such as a limited site or neighborhood reaction to the project can also help determine the design response. In every case, the journey the architect makes from the initial program statement to understanding what the client really needs gives its architecture shape.

FONTAINE HALL, MARIST COLLEGE
POUGHKEEPSIE, NEW YORK

Fontaine Hall contains three independent functions: the Humanities department offices and classrooms, the Marist Institute for Public Opinion (MIPO), and the offices of the College of Advancement. The building allows for an identity for each function, yet places primary importance on the Humanities department and its students. The site for this building is complex and a study in contrasts. To the west is a sweeping view of the Hudson River, while to the east is a busy thoroughfare with strip development. Students approach the building primarily from the existing campus to the south, while the north promises future expansion. Most dramatically, the building's site drops a full story from south to north.

The building's design accentuates this grade change, making the building's inhabitants aware of it as they move between its north and south ends. The glassy entrance tower collects visitors to the building from three directions. To the south, the tower provides a viewpoint from which one can witness the site rolling away to the north. This sudden contour change may surprise one, because it is effectively masked behind the building. Fontaine Hall meets the slope with a relentless colonnade that marches down the hill, growing taller and more powerful as it proceeds. Standing in the south lobby, one becomes aware of the building's movement across the site, and also of Fontaine Hall's height above the Hudson River to the west. In the upper spaces of the tower, windows frame views to the north, south, and west, offering other vantages of vistas around the building.

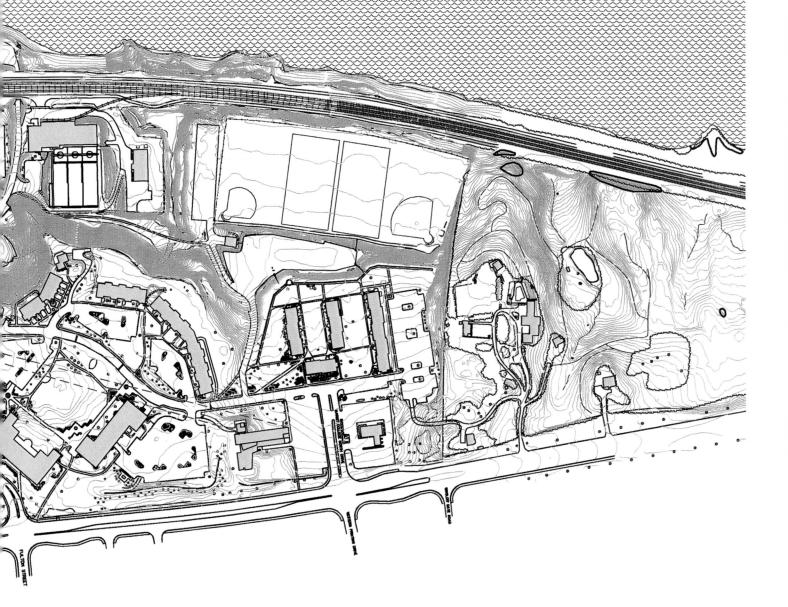

HUDSON RIVER

TOP   view from across river

BOTTOM   campus plan

132

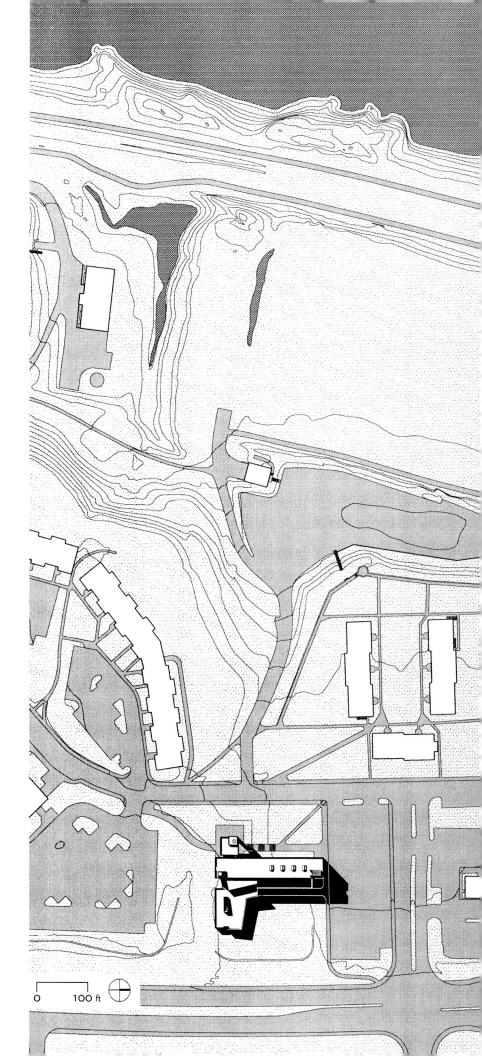

0   100 ft

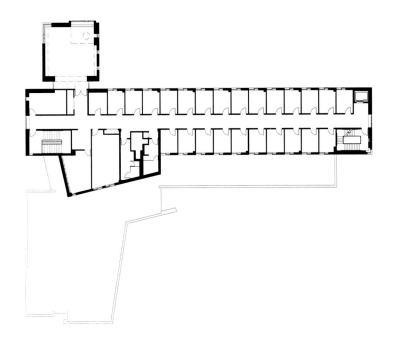

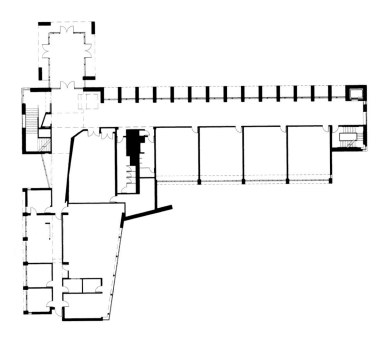

FACING PAGE   site plan

TOP   third floor plan

BOTTOM   first floor plan

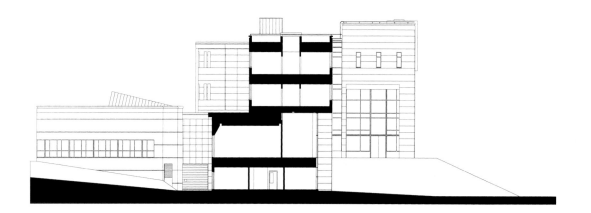

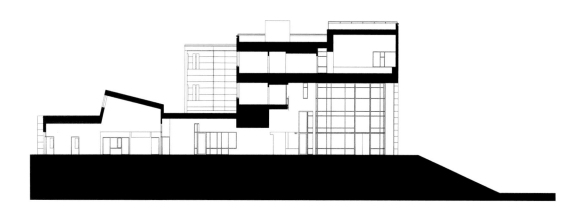

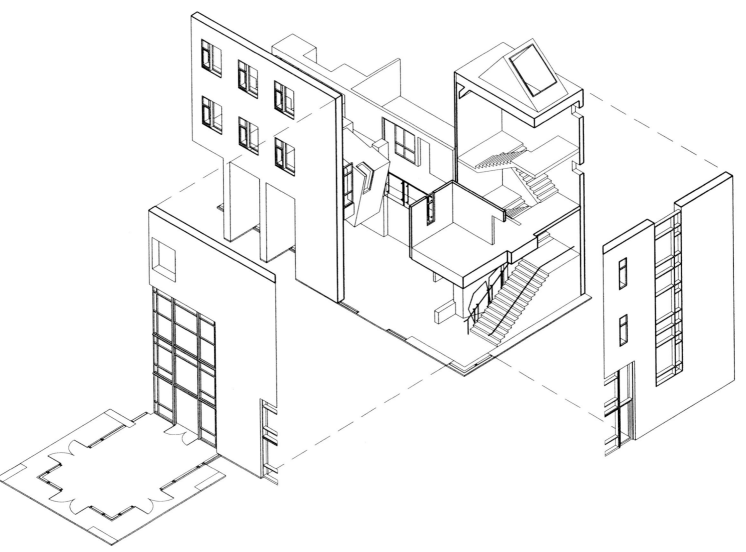

FACING PAGE TOP   west elevation

FACING PAGE MIDDLE   section at offices

FACING PAGE BOTTOM   section through entry and MIPO

ABOVE   exploded axonometric of entry

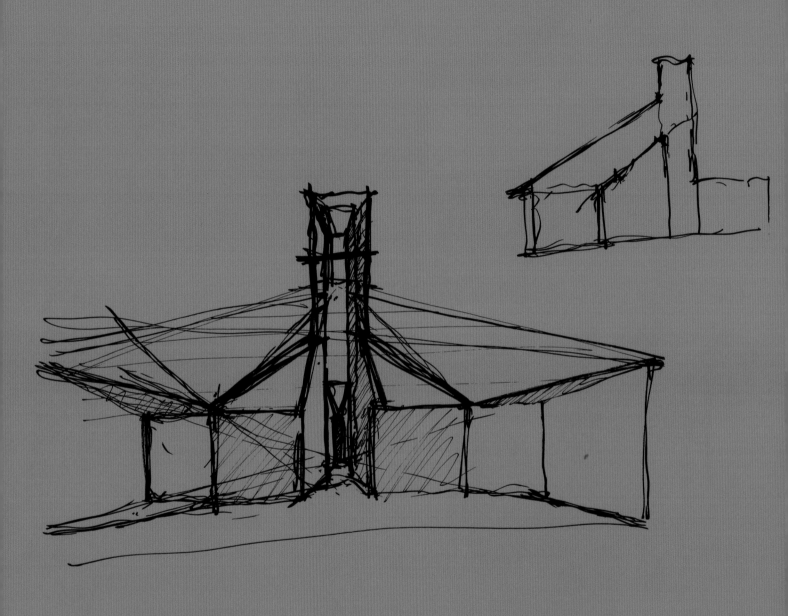

VISUAL ARTS CENTER, GROTON SCHOOL
GROTON, MASSACHUSETTS

The design of the Visual Arts Center at Groton School responds to the intimate scale and rich detail that exist on the campus. Yet the building has an identity all its own, which reflects the unique functions that occur within. It is a building whose design is driven by the programmatic needs of the study and creation of visual arts. The response to which determined building site, building form, and the manner in which natural light is manipulated.

The 13,000-square-foot building contains facilities for painting, drawing, printmaking, photography, and ceramics, as well as exhibition space for both professional and student work. The building is a single story organized around a series of 30 x 30 foot studios. The studios for two-dimensional study are located in a linear series with large north facing windows while the ceramics program is located in a separate wing of the building allowing it to receive light from multiple sides. The building has been designed with all of the studio spaces, as well as the exhibition space, on a single level so that each space can have tall ceilings and receive indirect top light through monitors and skylights. The monitors at the studios are glazed on all but the south side to prevent harsh southern light from entering the studios. The fourth side of the monitors has a dual purpose; from the exterior it serves the spaces mechanically and on the interior reflects light from the monitors down into the spaces. The hipped roof forms, which are capped with the monitors, result in a family of forms that are well suited to Groton School's existing roofscape.

142

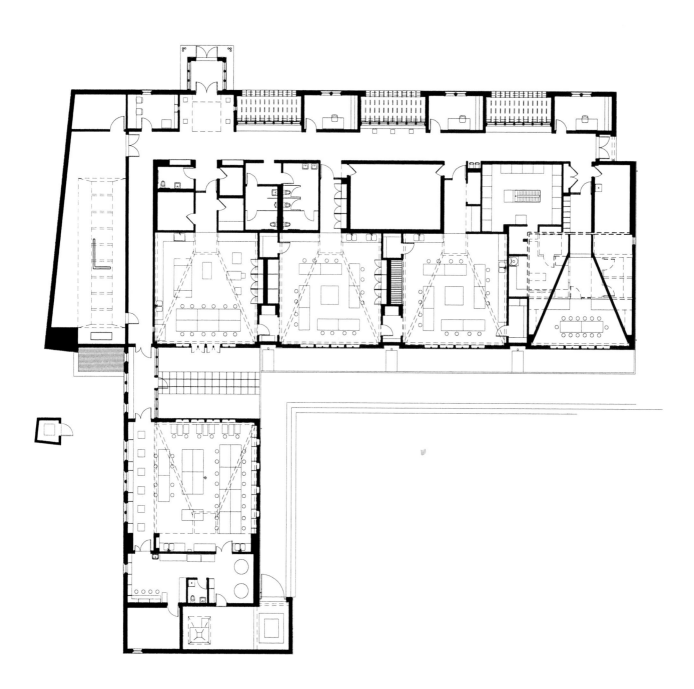

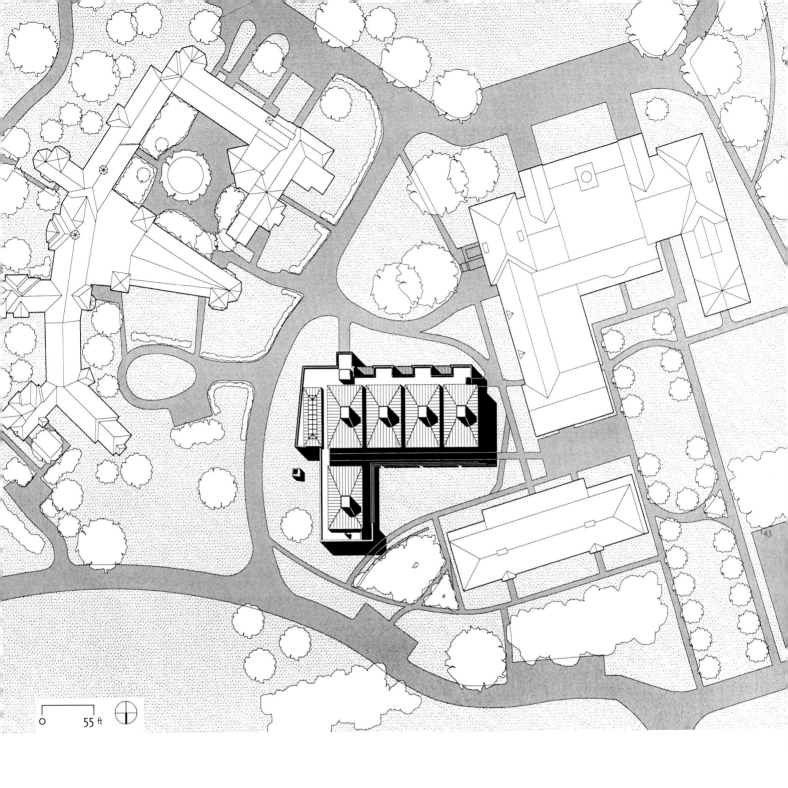

O   55 ft

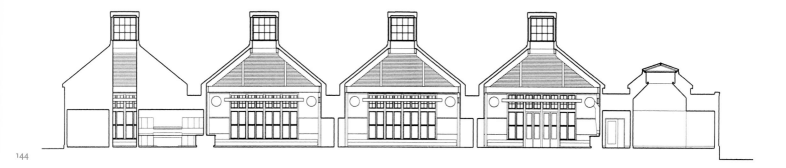

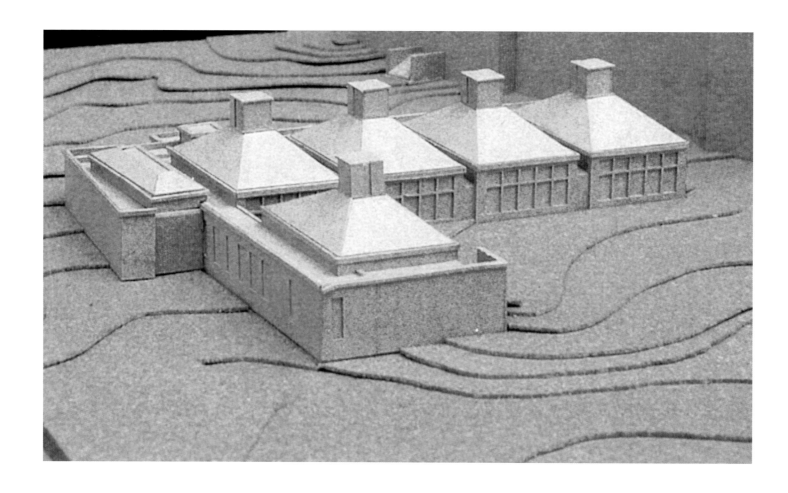

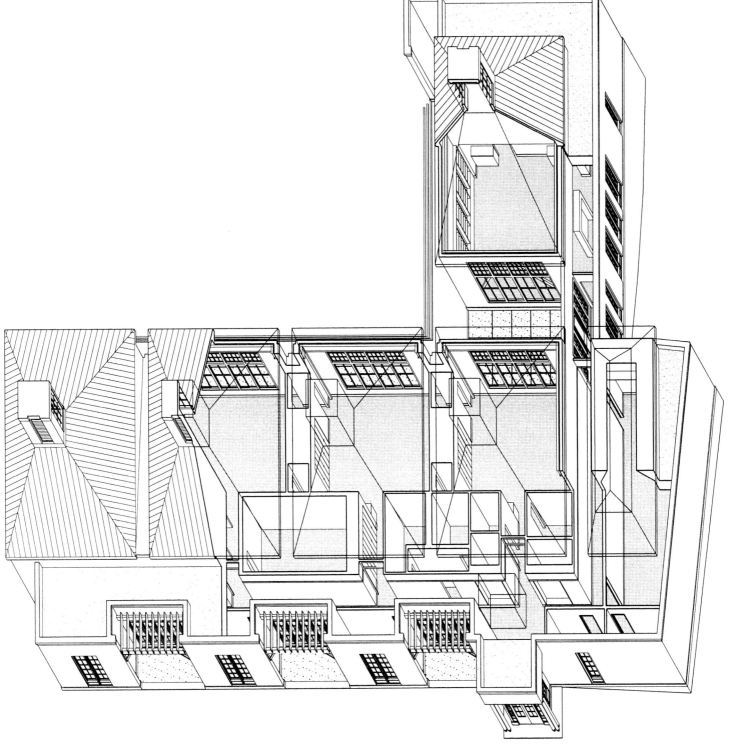

60 OXFORD STREET, HARVARD UNIVERSITY
CAMBRIDGE, MASSACHUSETTS

The site for 60 Oxford Street, an information systems building, is at the northernmost edge of Harvard's campus. At this point the campus abuts the late 19th century homes of the Agassiz neighborhood, a transition point from educational institution to residential enclave. Neither the community nor the university wanted an abrupt meeting of the two vastly different urban conditions. The design agenda was to transition from one context to another while maintaining Harvard's boundary and identity. The 95,000-square-foot program for the building, producing a footprint of more than 100' x 150', challenged this basic agenda. A typical house in the neighborhood, by contrast, has a footprint of less than $^1/_6$th of this area. The design solution organizes a series of building masses ranging in scale from a single story to four stories. These are composed to produce a series of landscape spaces around the building. As a result, the landscape itself provides continuity between the university and the neighborhood.

Although the composition emphasizes a small scale, the aggregation of elements allows for the 10,000-square-foot, uninterrupted floor plate of the data center.

The project also embraces a "green" building strategy. The deep footprint incorporates a central light well and large perimeter windows with light shelves to deliver light deep into the interior. A ventilated cavity "jalousie" window wall on the west elevation and a deep brise-soleil on the east elevation help control solar gain and glare.

Even with the conflicting agendas for the project, the building succeeds in creating a unified place out of a complex situation. It is a transitional building in the most literal sense, that is, a building that creates a passage from one place to another.

148

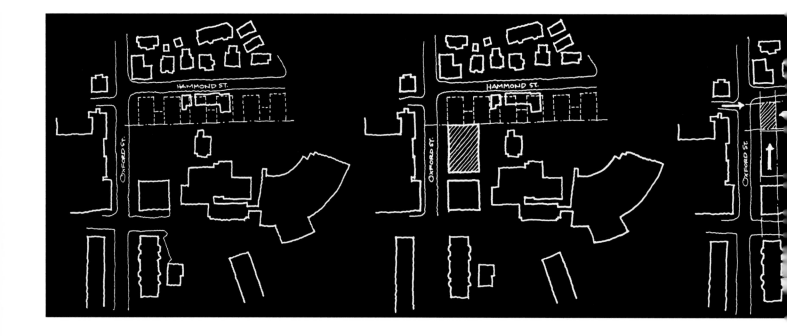

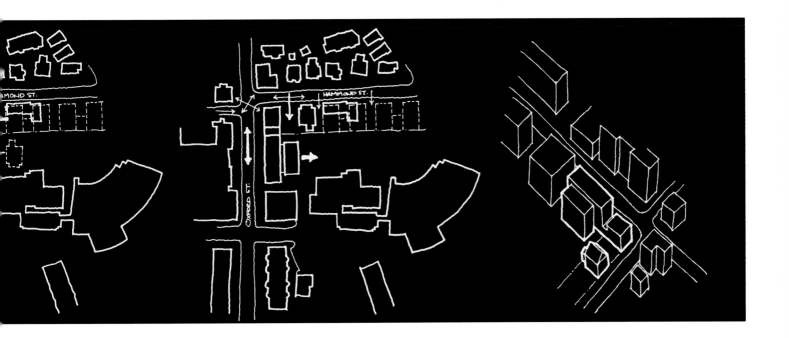

150

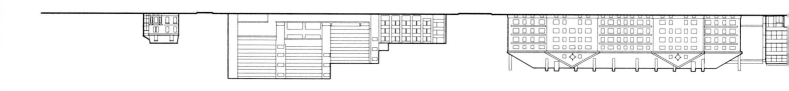

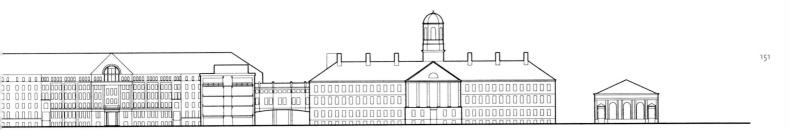

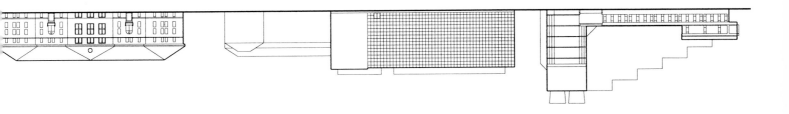

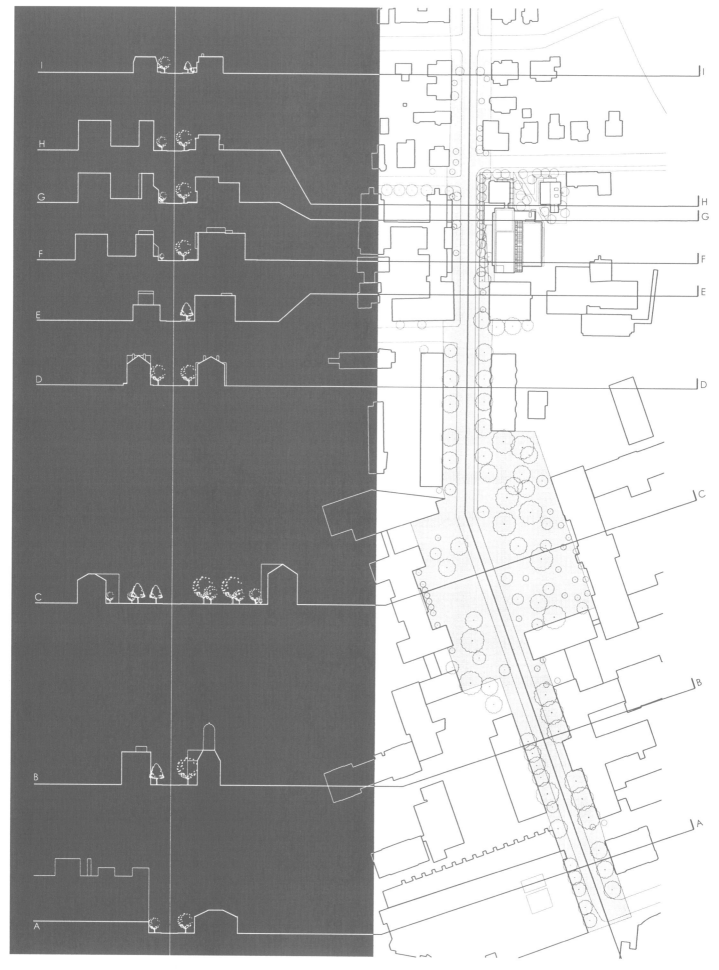

152

PROGRAM EFFECT

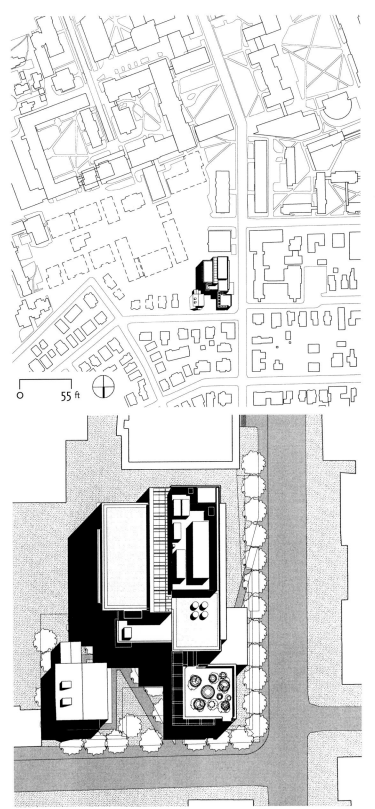

153

FACING PAGE   sectional studies of context and new building

TOP   site plan showing campus and neighborhood

BOTTOM   site plan

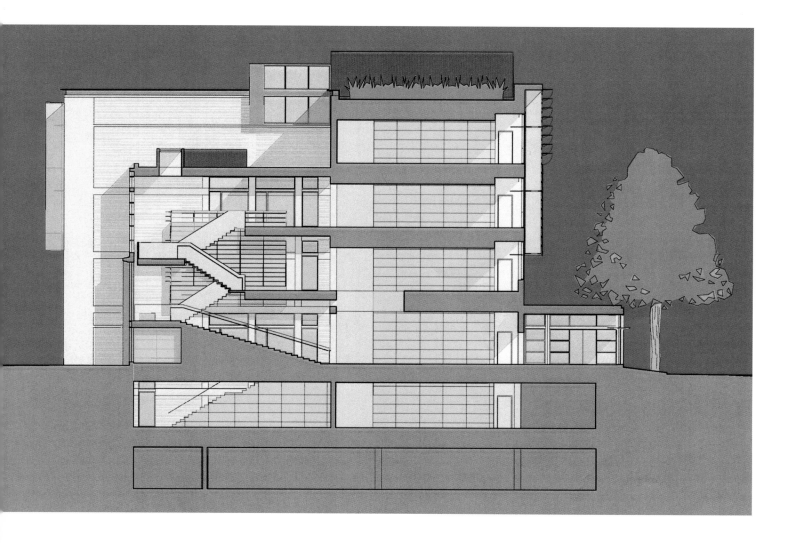

BELOW   section through roof garden

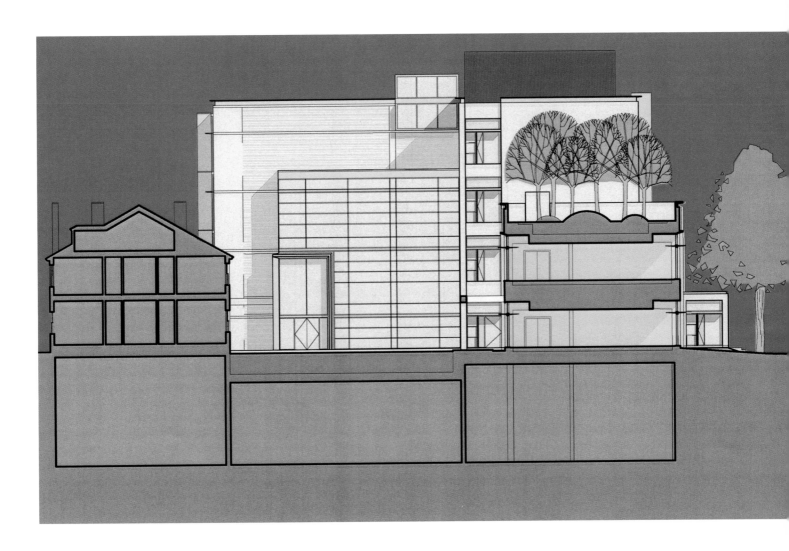

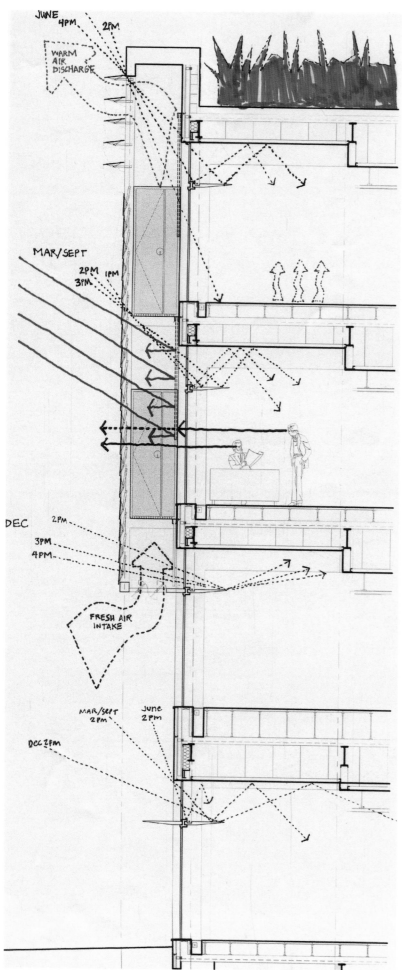

LEFT   analysis of light shading and natural ventilation

FACING PAGE   sectional study model showing sun-shading devices

JUNE
4PM   2PM

WARM
AIR
DISCHARGE

MAR/SEPT
2PM 1PM
3PM

DEC   2PM
3PM
4PM

FRESH AIR
INTAKE

MAR/SEPT
2PM

JUNE
2PM

DEC 2PM

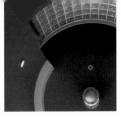

Of all of these categories of context, Episodic Monumentality perhaps comes closest to capturing how people, untrained in the discipline of architecture, experience the built environment on a day-to-day basis and interact with it. Here, the architect creates a series of loosely related "events" rendered in materials, color, shape, and light that become memorable in their ability to captivate, to suggest buildings recalled from personal history, to forge a community of people based on their previous architectural experiences.

The "episodic" nature of this condition bears fidelity to how we understand most of the environments we inhabit. There are generous numbers of inconsequential, "background" buildings that serve their functions well but do not rise to the level of a landmark. Interspersed within this buildingscape are monuments—civic, religious, or commercial—that mark our passage through space and make it memorable. They help us to position ourselves spatially within a continuum of buildings that may stretch miles in every direction. And they provide way-stations for meeting, shared understandings of what the built environment contains that allow us to fix upon it as a place to gather and share community.

Episodic Monumentality exploits the way we experience the built world. It can condense it within a single building, offering a series of seemingly unrelated points of reference that for us become landmarks that we use to move around the building. It also offers the element of surprise, the "wow" factor that all great architecture possesses. Occasionally, Episodic Monumentality provides an opportunity for delight and humor in the built environment.

HEALTH SCIENCES AND HUMAN SERVICES LIBRARY, UNIVERSITY OF MARYLAND, BALTIMORE

BALTIMORE, MARYLAND

The University of Maryland Health Sciences and Human Services Library occupies a full city block on the eastern edge of its campus. Holding and defining its site, this 190,000-square-foot building has a strong urban presence. It is rendered in lasting materials of brick, limestone, and steel. The building's visual weight, however, is reduced with the measured use of light-colored stone on its principal facades. These same materials are seen in the library's surrounding context, and the new ties tightly to the existing urban fabric.

The library's plan is rational yet full of surprises. The rectilinear frame on four of the six floors contains book stacks at its center, with a variety of seating at the periphery. The figural tower alternates as study space, lounge, classroom, and demonstration space. The west side houses administrative space, computers, and other library services. At the very heart of the library is its most monumental space—a dramatic staircase that rises four stories in continuous runs, so that one can stand at the bottom of the stairs and look straight up to the fifth floor. The staircase is a powerful, unifying device that stitches the multitude of library spaces together. It helps to orient the visitor who can easily move from one level to another. And it becomes an important social space, where people meet while moving through the library. Throughout, strong colors vibrate and enliven the interior, particularly a curving red wall at the entry that splays to reveal the grand flight of stairs and rises with it.

DESIGN ARCHITECT: PERRY DEAN ROGERS | PARTNERS ARCHITECTS
ASSOCIATED ARCHITECT: DESIGN COLLECTIVE, INC. OF BALTIMORE

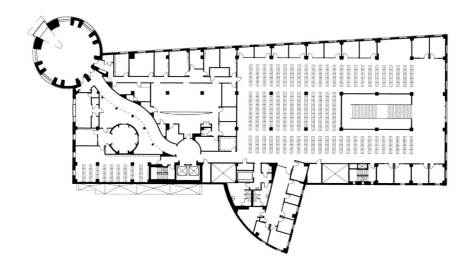

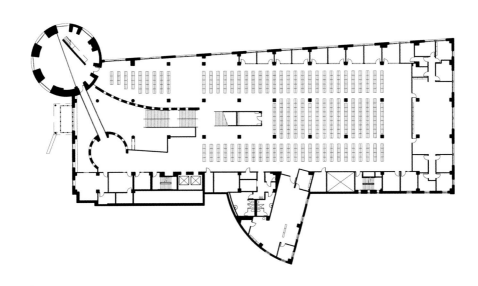

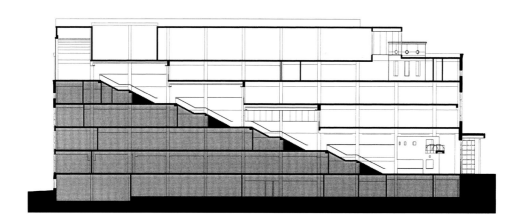

FACING PAGE TOP   fifth floor plan

FACING PAGE MIDDLE   first floor plan

FACING PAGE BOTTOM   longitudinal section

BELOW   site plan illustrating relationship to historic
Davidge Hall

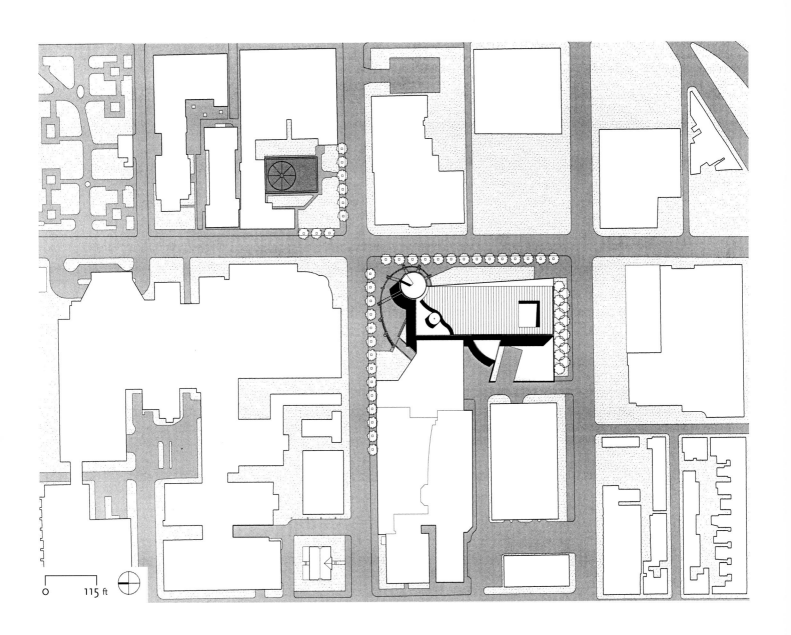

O ⊢——⊣ 115 ft

FACING PAGE TOP   desk with openings to lobby

FACING PAGE BOTTOM   monumental stair

TOP   opening detail

BOTTOM   main entrance lobby

CAMPUS MASTER PLAN, MILTON HERSHEY SCHOOL
HERSHEY, PENNSYLVANIA

Creating a memorable outdoor space, one in which students would feel welcome and part of a community, is the goal of this design. The new campus plan creates a new center of gravity for the school. To make this central space memorable, the architects drew upon elements that are part of the collective memory of those who attend the school.

The school includes a visual and performing arts center, with museum-quality gallery space, a learning resource center, a gymnasium with seating for 1,792, a middle school, a high school, and renovations to convert the existing middle school to a campus center and administration building. These facilities form a new, more centralized campus, allowing a community gathering space for teaching and social events ranging from outdoor painting and sculpture to poetry readings to graduation ceremonies and other important functions.

Not far from the campus in this Pennsylvania farm community, large barns stand like sentinels in fields, and the new designs capture their monumental quality. The use of stone and clapboard, recalled from the materials of the neighboring barns, helps to establish a sense of shared architecture in form and material.

The Visual Arts building is a sculptural event in its own right on the path leading to the school's new "village green." The 300-foot-wide circular open space of the green not only gives the campus a focal point that it previously lacked, but it also serves as a foreground for individual landmark architectural elements, such as the clock tower at the threshold of the space, the tall porches, and the cupolas that crown the roof lines. Around the circle, these events become a new collection of memories for Hershey's students.

BELOW   high school with clock tower marking major arrival point

FACING PAGE TOP   high school northwest elevation

FACING PAGE MIDDLE   multipurpose gymnasium south elevation

FACING PAGE BOTTOM   multipurpose gymnasium west elevation

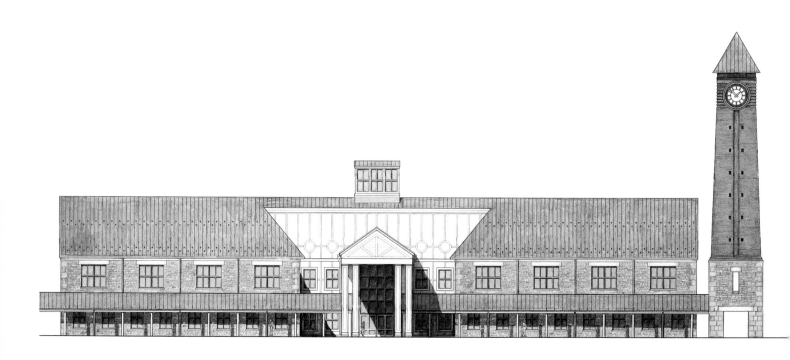

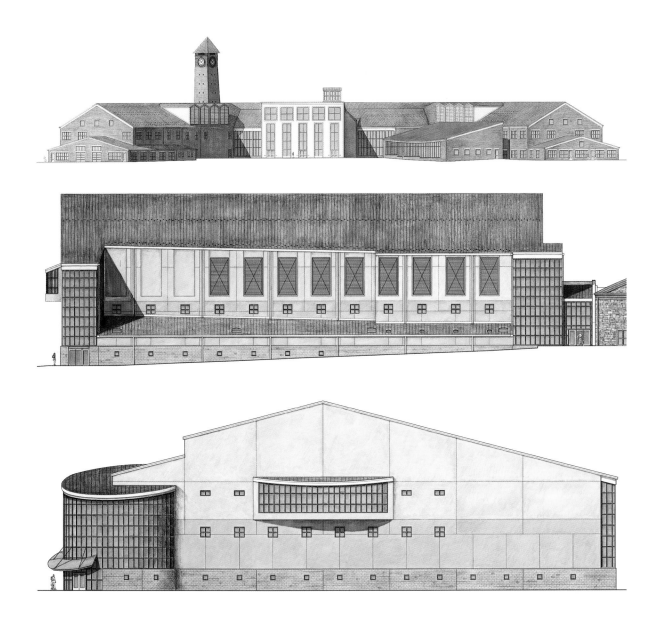

178   TOP   north elevation with section through connecting bridge

MIDDLE   south elevation

BOTTOM   longitudinal section through display corridor

FACING PAGE   axonometrics of visual arts center

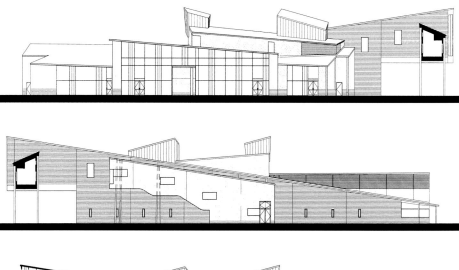

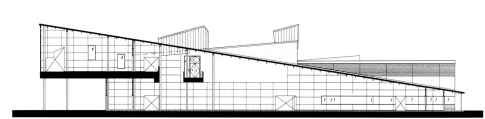

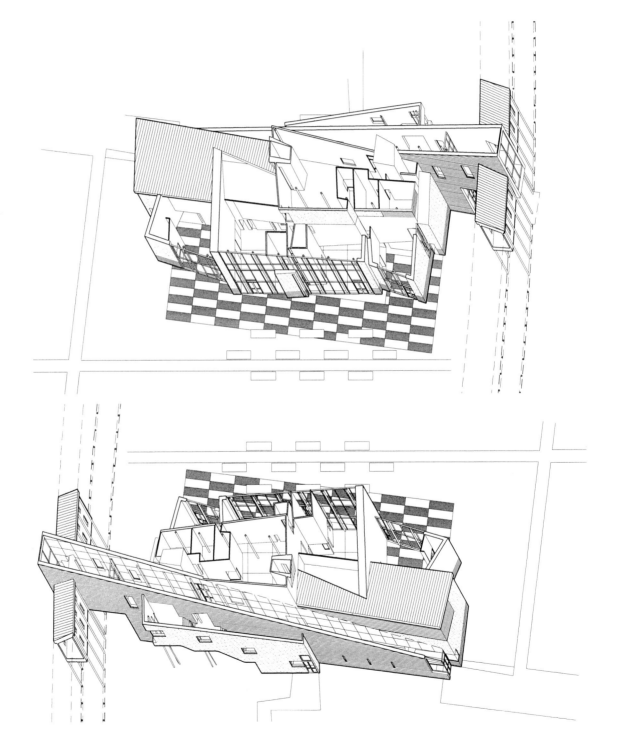

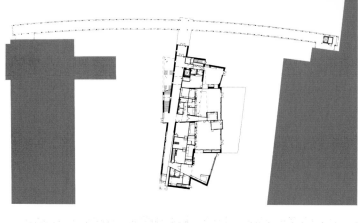

LEFT   first floor plan of visual arts center

MIDDLE   second floor plan of visual arts center

RIGHT   connecting bridge floor plan of visual arts center

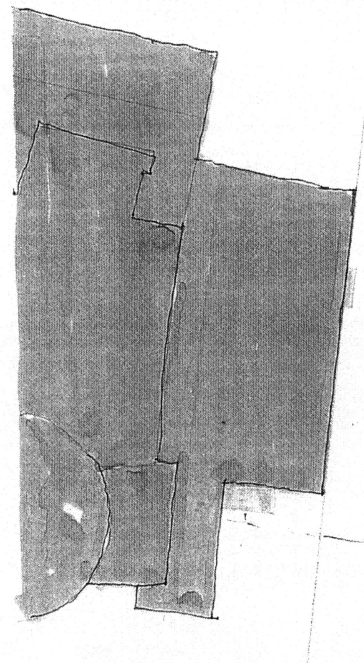

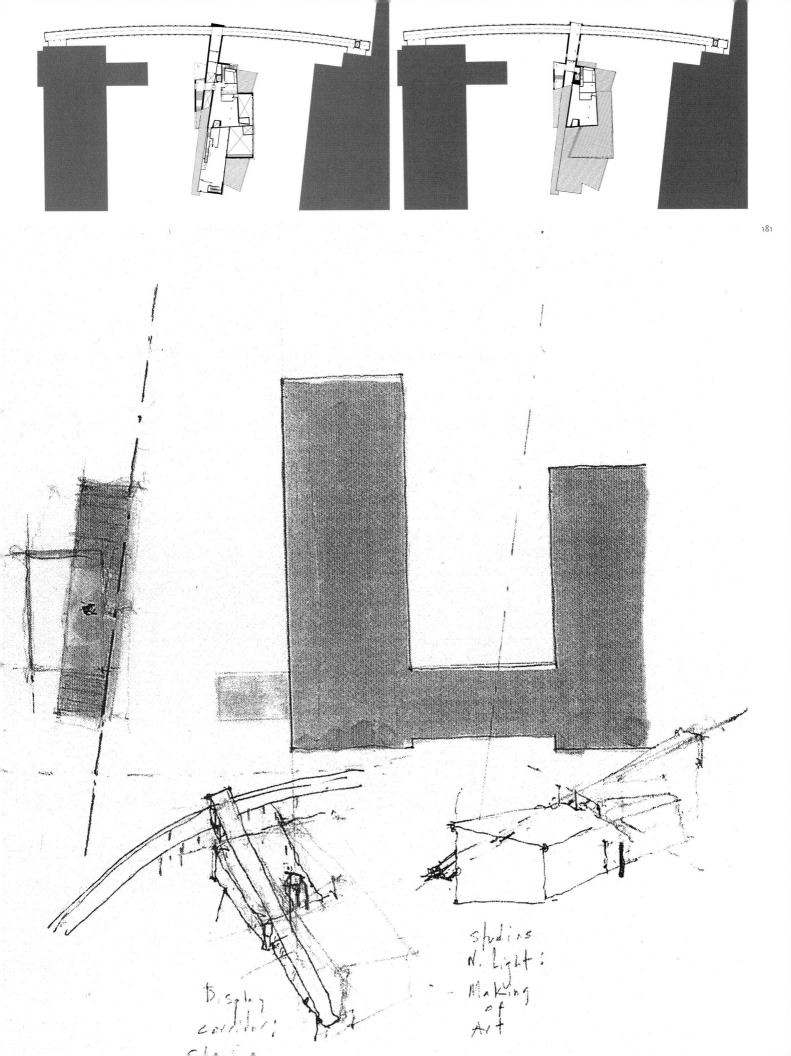

Display
corridor:

studios
N. Light:
Making
of
Art

FLO K. GAULT LIBRARY OF INDEPENDENT STUDY, COLLEGE OF WOOSTER
WOOSTER, OHIO

The Flo K. Gault Library addition to Andrews Library at the College of Wooster makes a strong new link to the campus plan. Andrews Library, built in the 1960s, is clad in limestone in an austere, classical style. This symmetrical, three-story, rectangular building is longest along its north-south axis, with entrances on the east and west facades. To the north is Memorial Walk, a major pedestrian route that links many of the campus buildings.

The college is distinguished by its Independent Study Program, which requires seniors to complete a written thesis for graduation. One of the goals for the new library was to accommodate students in their pursuit of independent study. The other was to express this program architecturally as an important feature of the college. The architects have done both by filling Gault and Andrews with nearly 300 independent study carrels, and by creating an important new landmark for the college. The new building is the same height and width as Andrews, and is clad in the same limestone skin, with cornices, molding, and other exterior details from the existing library. A dramatic departure from Andrews is found on Gault's north wall, which addresses Memorial Walk. The limestone walls pull apart and between them rises a three-story, faceted, glass wall that displays Gault's interior. In front of this crystaline curtain wall are a glassy clock tower that holds the library's new entrance and a circular stair that curls from the second to third floor, where study carrels may be seen at the balconies' edges. The exterior form and materials of the Gault addition are examples of the architects' most sensitive and inventive uses of contextual design.

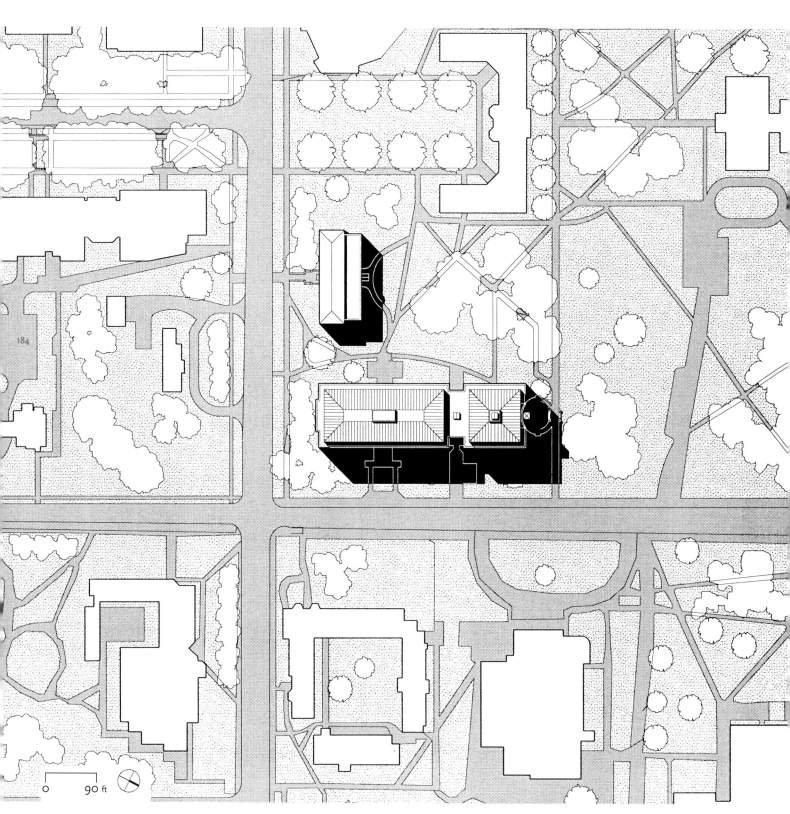

0   90 ft

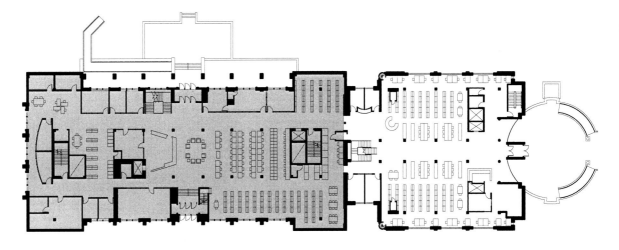

FACING PAGE   site plan showing Gault and Timken Science Library

TOP   first floor plan with existing shaded

BOTTOM   section through Gault addition

LEFT   interior detail at curtainwall

RIGHT   entry hall

FACING PAGE   transparent north elevation

An existing structure brings an immediate, palpable, and measurable context to any architectural addition or intervention. In spite of this surplus of contextual material, any addition is necessarily an interpretation (explanatory or conceptual) of the given conditions. An addition is, by definition, an appendage to an original structure.

The intention is not the subordination of the new, but fostering a conversation between new needs and old circumstances. This approach should demonstrate the architect's restraint; tempered with new approaches that do not deny the time and place in which they are created. An evolutionary approach to the built environment suggests a selective strategy in which the hand of the new architect is revealed, while still respecting the work of those who have come before. This approach requires a critical, open interpretation of the given conditions, while recognizing that there are built-in limits to any interpretation. The method is open to discovery, where the designer actively interprets the given conditions and generates a solution that selectively employs the existing context.

Such projects are especially challenging within the context of a strong existing building, by past masters such as Alvar Aalto or the early 20th century American architect James Gamble Rogers, whose creations in a sense become the "site" for the Addition Intervention.

FINE ARTS CENTER LOBBY, UNIVERSITY OF MASSACHUSETTS
AMHERST, MASSACHUSETTS

The Fine Arts Center, designed by Roche Dinkeloo in the 1960s, lacked a clearly identifiable entrance and theater spill-out space. The challenge was to mend these design deficiencies in the spirit of this brutalist style building. The solution is a new lobby that occupies former outdoor plaza space, connecting the Rand Theater, the Concert Hall, and the Fine Arts Center (existing gallery space is below the lobby). The new lobby is also a gateway to the campus beyond and provides a visual landmark that identifies the Fine Arts Center.

Concrete and lead-coated copper are the dominant materials of the original building. In clear contrast, the new lobby is a rectangular assemblage of transparent and translucent glass—a delicate light box inserted between two massive opaque volumes. Three glass boxes of varying size create a transparent link between the upper and lower campus, as well as knit together the disparate volumes of the Concert Hall and the Rand Theater. The lobby's structural framework is clad in lead-coated copper.

Instead of overt signage, light and color are used as design elements to provide an identity to this enigmatic structure. Suspended lanterns of plaster funnel natural light from above into the lobby space. The lanterns are painted in primary colors of red and yellow to effectively project pigmented shadows onto the surfaces of the interior space. At night, gelled lights fill the glass boxes with saturated colors of blue, red, green, orange, and violet, which fade in and out, creating a mysterious beacon to attract visitors.

194

196

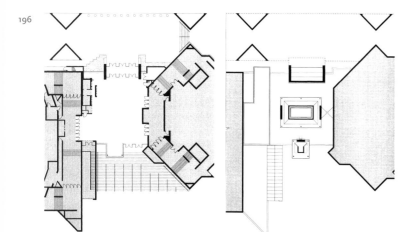

LEFT   plan at lobby level with existing shaded

BELOW   concept drawing

RIGHT   plan at lantern level with existing shaded

BELOW   section through new lobby

BOTTOM   detail of interior lantern

FACING PAGE   suspended lantern captures light and

reflects color

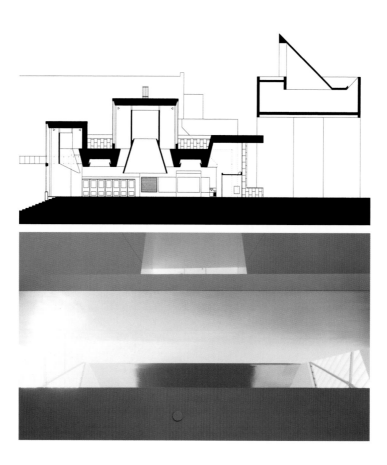

ABOVE details showing juxtaposition of clear glass and
translucent cast glass

BRANFORD AND SAYBROOK COLLEGES, YALE UNIVERSITY
NEW HAVEN, CONNECTICUT

Designed in 1917 by James Gamble Rogers, Harkness Quadrangle, which includes Branford and Saybrook Colleges and the 250-foot-tall Harkness Tower, is one of Yale's largest residential complexes. Robert Frost once noted that Branford was the most beautiful of Yale's residential colleges, but by the late 1990s, the buildings had fallen into disrepair. The new design brings the complex into the 21st century.

The renovation includes the minor reconfiguration of existing suites of rooms in order to increase the bed count from 409 to 552. It also includes a complete overhaul of the dining rooms, common rooms, and libraries. A two-story building at Calliope court was reconceived as the Branford library, carving away spaces to expose fireplaces and a curving stair. A new vaulted ceiling captures light from attic windows for the second floor mezzanine. Rogers did not design the basement for occupancy. In the new plan, the basement is conceived of as an urban street linking together nodes of student activities--such as game rooms, the "buttery" (a student-run kitchen), exercise rooms, theaters, TV lounges, and renovated squash courts –with colors and textures drawing the path.

All of the new additions and interventions are achieved within the confines of Rogers's original building envelope. The buildings are narrow bars of space only 32 feet wide, with simple structural systems that allow for the insertion of new uses. The design accommodates these new functions while also exploiting the three-dimensional potential of the buildings, permitting them to be experienced in a variety of ways.

206

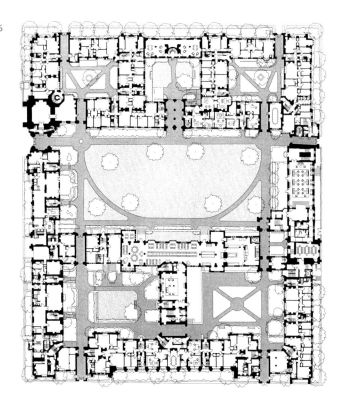

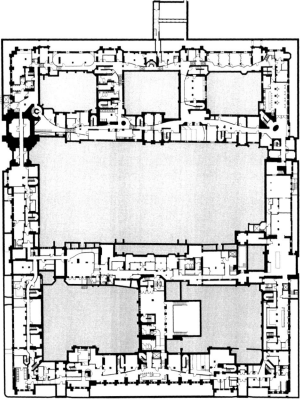

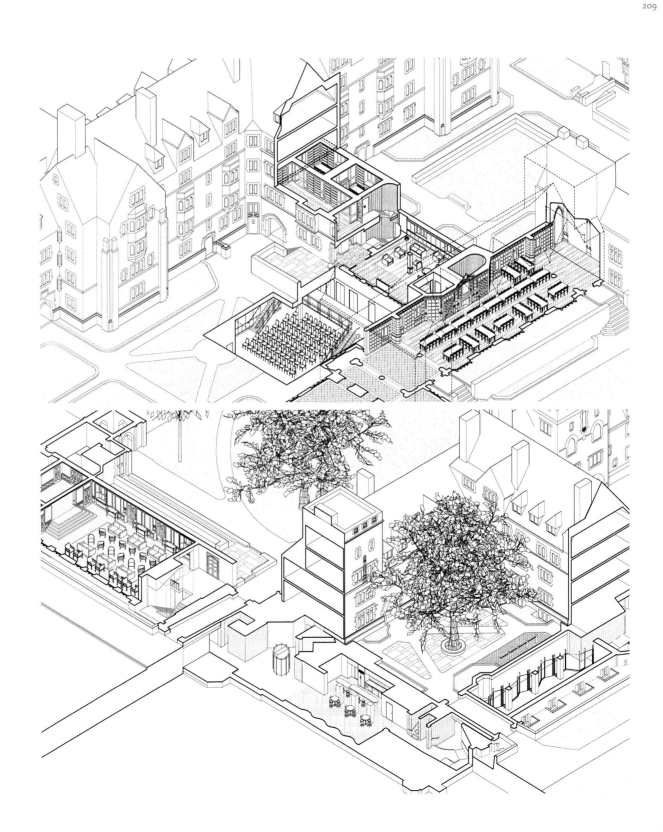

BELOW   sectional axonometric of newly created library
within existing shell
FACING PAGE   new library

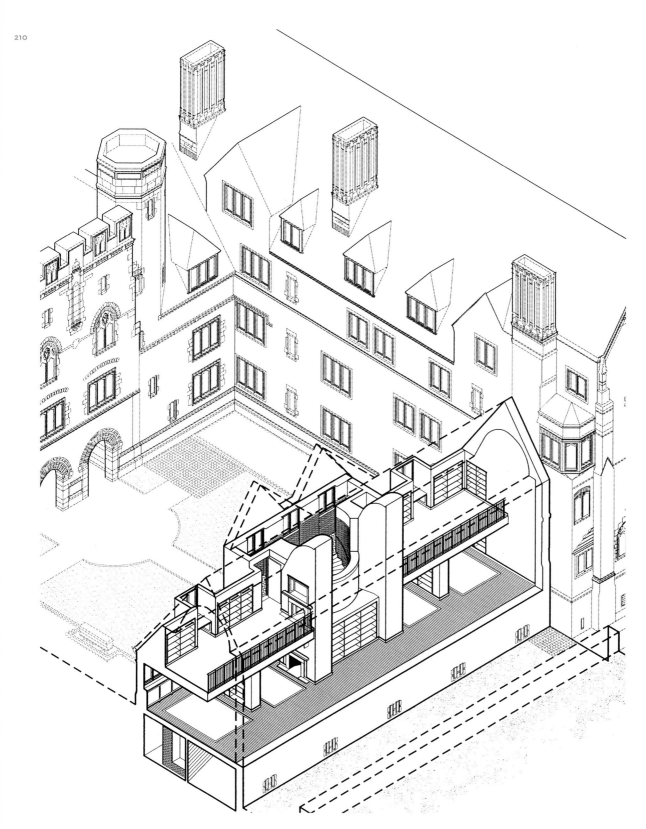

STEWART M. REID OFFICE OF ADMISSIONS, WESLEYAN UNIVERSITY
MIDDLETOWN, CONNECTICUT

Situated at the marriage of two grids—one of the Wesleyan University campus, the other of the town of Middletown, Connecticut— this project creates a vantage point from which both may be experienced, and the Wesleyan campus explained to incoming students and their families. The project involves the renovation of an existing residence and the addition of approximately 10,000 square feet of new space. Most of the program spaces of the Admissions building align with the city grid, while the building's Great Room (used as the University's "living room" to welcome students)

aligns with the grain of the campus proper. As an intermediary, the building reinforces its relationship to both areas of the surrounding context, featuring long views to vital areas of the main campus to the south as well as to the Center for the Arts to the north.

On the exterior, one becomes aware of these two external forces through the new building's geometry. On one level it is faithfully at right angles to the existing residence. But the new addition's wrapper cranks slightly to reveal a skewed wall, which picks up on the other grid. This becomes most apparent in the shallow eave that wraps around the corner

and terminates in the fireplace mass.

On the interior, the building's coveted spot on campus is revealed when one stands in the "living room" space, which is wrapped in large windows that offer views up and down the campus. From here, the Wesleyan campus grid unfolds, the new building acting as a pivot revealing the tension of the two intersecting grids.

ABOVE   section through addition

BELOW   site and building plan with existing shaded

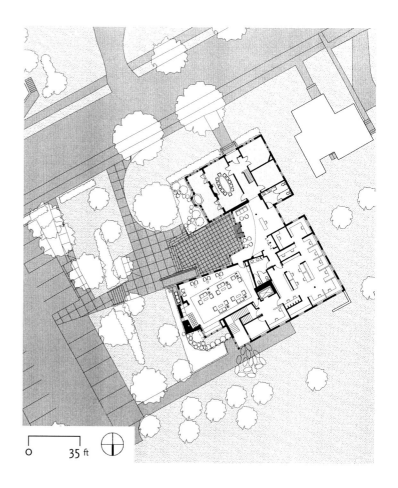

0   35 ft

TIMKEN SCIENCE LIBRARY, COLLEGE OF WOOSTER
WOOSTER, OHIO

The new Timken Science Library is in the oldest building on campus. Nesting new within old became a theme in the design, where a new staircase and shelving are expressed in a crisp, modernist esthetic, while the building's classical columns and cornices are meticulously restored.

Frick Hall, as it was dedicated in 1900, served as the university library for 62 years, until the completion of Andrews Library nearby. With the expansion of Andrews with the new Flo K. Gault Library, Frick was pressed back into service to house the college's scattered natural sciences collection. The science collection is 35,000 volumes, and the original building's structure could not support compact shelving. The stack wing to the north was gutted and a new, freestanding, three-story structure was built inside it, allowing light to penetrate to the previously unlit second floor. Compact shelves are on the lowest level with two stories of conventional stacks above. Marble columns and an elaborate architrave distinguish Timken's beautifully restored main reading room. Two columns were added, which conceal heating, ventilation, and air conditioning ductwork and complete the original set of reading room columns. At the west and east ends of the room are freestanding mezzanines with study carrels on top and periodicals below. These structures are rendered in clean, crisp materials (white panelling, frosted glass, and stainless steel) that identify them as new additions.

The original south-facing library entrance opened directly into the second level reading room. This entrance was recreated on the ground floor to allow full accessibility. In addition, the campus had grown to the north, so a new entrance, on what had been the building's backside, was created of limestone, metal, and glass.

BELOW transverse section through north and south
entrances
BOTTOM longitudinal section through restored reading room
FACING PAGE exploded axonometric illustrating nesting
concept

218

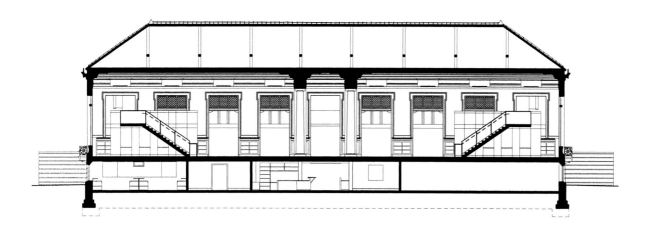

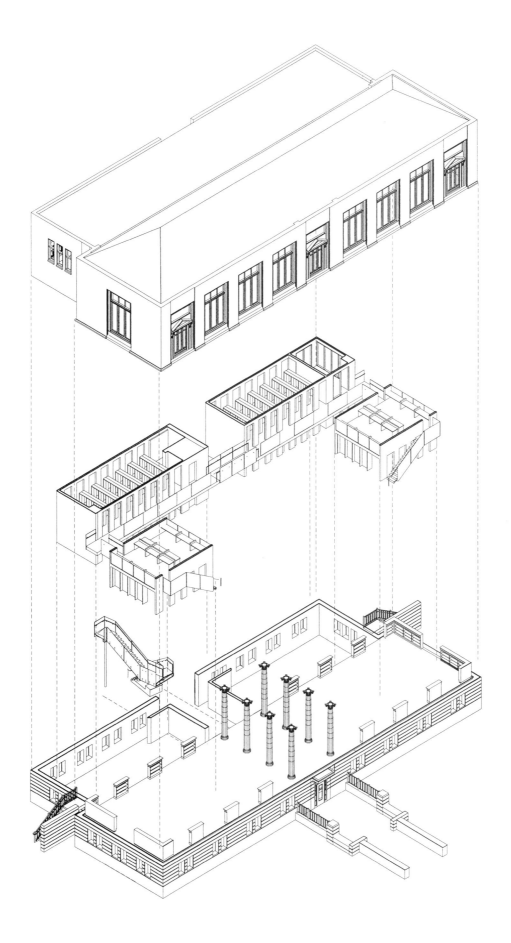

220

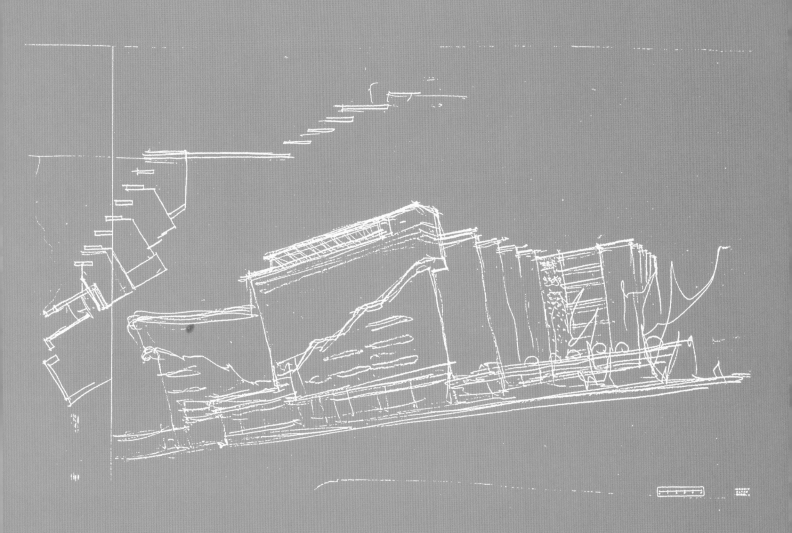

BAKER HOUSE DORMITORY, MASSACHUSETTS INSTITUTE OF TECHNOLOGY
CAMBRIDGE, MASSACHUSETTS

Baker House Dormitory, designed in 1947 by world-renowned Finnish architect Alvar Aalto, is one of the seminal Modern buildings in North America, and one of only two Aalto buildings in the U.S. Perry Dean Rogers and Partners approached the task of a comprehensive restoration and upgrade to prepare Baker for the next 50 years of active student life by studying Aalto's architecture and making enlightened design decisions faithful to the intent of the original architect. In fact, Perry Dean Rogers and Partners had an early connection to Baker House: The firm provided Aalto space in its Boston office when he was working on the original design, and helped prepare the working drawings.

Programmatically, the project required a complete renovation and upgrade of kitchen and dining facilities; new activity areas such as a game room, TV room, group and individual study areas, a workshop, conference room, music room, and fitness center; refurbished student lounge areas, including new and recaptured lounge space; a new entry lobby; upgrades to student rooms; and the complete integration of mechanical, electrical, plumbing, fire protection, telecommunication, and security systems throughout the building. Roof-top recreational space was also added.

Visiting Aalto's studio in Helsinki, and studying the Baker House drawings, sketches, details, and correspondence, as well as Aalto designs from the same period, allowed the architects to interpret Aalto's intentions when considering new additions to Baker. For example, new trellises on the roof at the entry—elements Aalto had intended in the original design—were developed following his sketches.

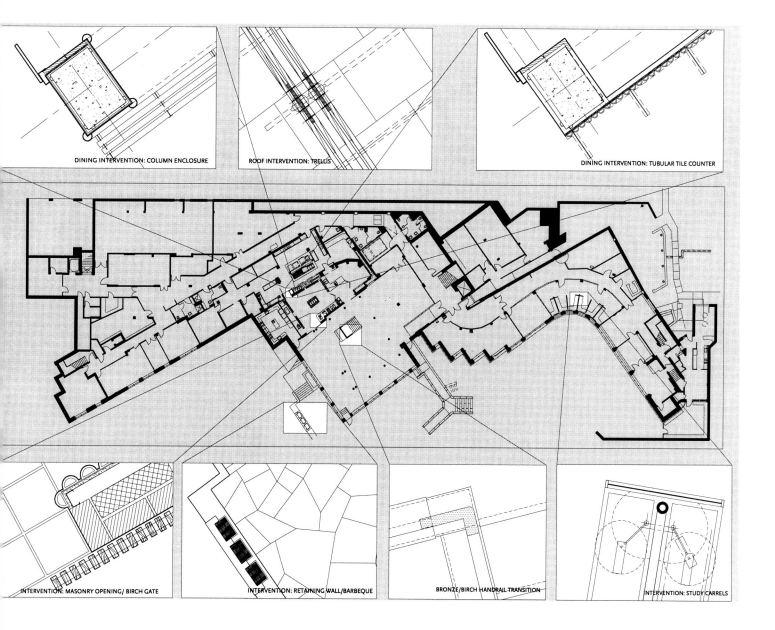

DINING INTERVENTION: COLUMN ENCLOSURE

ROOF INTERVENTION: TRELLIS

DINING INTERVENTION: TUBULAR TILE COUNTER

INTERVENTION: MASONRY OPENING/ BIRCH GATE

INTERVENTION: RETAINING WALL/BARBEQUE

BRONZE/BIRCH HANDRAIL TRANSITION

INTERVENTION: STUDY CARRELS

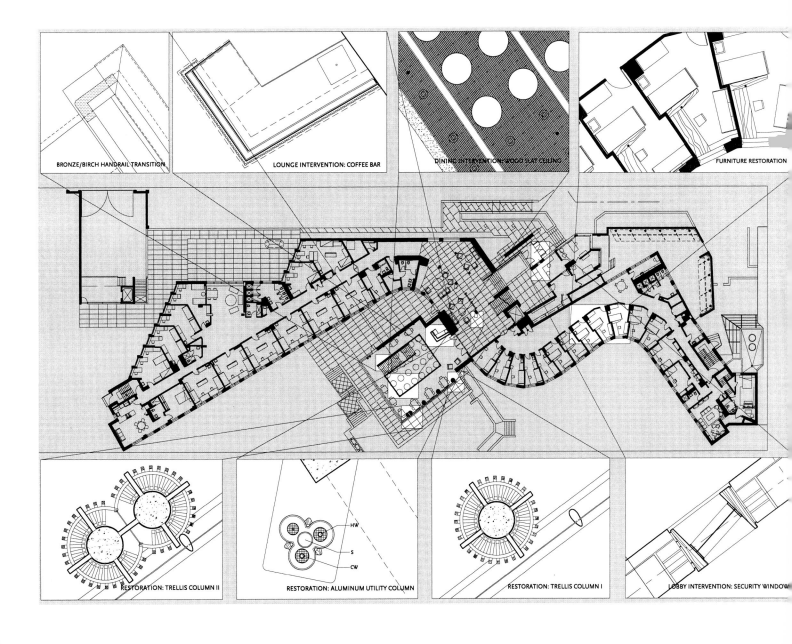

BRONZE/BIRCH HANDRAIL TRANSITION

LOUNGE INTERVENTION: COFFEE BAR

DINING INTERVENTION: WOOD SLAT CEILING

FURNITURE RESTORATION

RESTORATION: TRELLIS COLUMN II

RESTORATION: ALUMINUM UTILITY COLUMN

HW

S

CW

RESTORATION: TRELLIS COLUMN I

LOBBY INTERVENTION: SECURITY WINDOW

226

LEFT   roof trellises complete original Aalto design

MIDDLE   new study carrels

RIGHT   upper balcony of moon garden dining restoration

FACING PAGE   restored lounge space with originally specified Aalto furniture

FOLLOWING PAGES   dining room stair to moon garden balcony

226

226

ADDITIONS INTERVENTIONS

PRINCIPALS

Steven M. Foote
Martha A. Pilgreen
Peter A. Ringenbach
Charles F. Rogers

SENIOR ASSOCIATES

James Bennette Jr.
Frank Chirico
Ned Collier
Thomas McCarty
Warren VanWees
Michael Waters

ASSOCIATES

Mark Allen
Gregory Burchard
Danyul Cho
Jeffrey Fishbein
Tracy Frederico
Gerard Gutierrez
Bryan Irwin
Anne Johnson
Christopher Scovel

COLLABORATORS 1996-2001

Jennifer Akerman
Mary-Ann Agresti
Jessica Anderson
Anat Banin
Alessandra Basseto
John Berg
Elizabeth Bloomer
Andrew Brockway
Jeffrey Brouse
Marshall Brown
Sherri Bruce
Rachel Campbell
Gail Cavanagh
Yun Chan
Alan Christ
David Coe
Greg Colling
Nicholas Connors
Christine Curran
Kevin Deabler
Alicia Dembro
Douglas Dick

Brian DiRusso
Mark Dolny
Daniel Dwyer
Kimberly Elliott
Laurie Fanger
Caryn Finn-Reilly
Mark Freeman
Ana Gabby
Daniel Gallagher
Adam Gilmore
Melissa Gorman
Richard Greene
Cathy Hahn
Leekyung Han
Heather Herbert
Julie Thomas Hess
John Hollister
Hiromi Hosoya
Bruce Hutt
Walter Jacob
Richard Jones
Amanda Josephs
Theresa Kelley
Lisa Kelly
Donald Knowles
Janet Kozun
Grace La
Kim-Yen Lai-Nguyen
J. William Lassetter
Valerie Legagneur
Kathleen Lenihan
Ashley Long
Neil Martin
Janis McClinch
Nancy McDonald
Francis McGuire
Julia McMorrough
Jennifer Mondello
James Moore
Timothy Mulligan
Cynthia Munch
Anne Myers
Michael Oldakowski
Svetlana Ordian
Michael O'Connell
Samantha Pearson

Randolph Pease
Christopher Pitman
Elizabeth Porzio
Elaine Powers
Bradford Prestbo
Zachary Provonchee
Timothy Quirk
Toby Rand
Marissa Recor
Adam Redbord
Patricia Rhee
Robert Rink
Donald Roche
Alkistis Rodi
Jennifer Sarabia
Henry Scollard
Henry Sedelmaier
Jeannette Schram
Kari Silloway
Jessica Silver
Scott Slarsky
Janet Smith
Alejandro Soto
Peter Spaulding
Olga St. Clair
Eric Stark
Gary Stein
Brent Stringfellow
David Suvak
Mark Taber
Joan Tommy
Jennifer Tucker
Allison Walker
Gregory Walker
Meredith Wambsgans
Kathleen Wilson
Mark Wintringer
Kathy Wislocky
Jeffrey Wolff

CREDITS

DICKINSON COLLEGE
Richard Mandelkorn *photographs*

MARSHALL UNIVERSITY
Richard Mandelkorn *photographs*

MOUNT UNION COLLEGE
Anne Gummerson *photographs*

COLORADO STATE UNIVERSITY
Timothy Hursley *photographs*
Mary-Ann Agresti *furniture and furnishings*

SHADY HILL SCHOOL
Dan Bibb *photographs*

UNIVERSITY OF MARYLAND, BALTIMORE COUNTY
Mary-Ann Agresti *furniture and furnishings*

MARIST COLLEGE
Richard Mandelkorn *photographs*

HARVARD UNIVERSITY
Robert Comazzi *watercolor rendering*

UNIVERSITY OF MARYLAND, BALTIMORE
Anne Gummerson *photographs*

MILTON HERSHEY SCHOOL
Robert Comazzi *site plan rendering*

COLLEGE OF WOOSTER, FLO K GAULT LIBRARY
Robert Shimer/Hedrick Blessing *photographs*

UNIVERSITY OF MASSACHUSETTS
Peter Mauss/ESTO *photographs*
Dan Bibb *photographs pg. 200 and 202 (2nd and 3rd from left)*

YALE UNIVERSITY
Richard Mandelkorn *photographs*
Mary-Ann Agresti *furniture and furnishings*

WESLEYAN UNIVERSITY
Richard Mandelkorn *photographs*

COLLEGE OF WOOSTER, TIMKEN SCIENCE LIBRARY
Robert Shimer/Hedrick Blessing *photographs*

MASSACHUSETTS INSTITUTE OF TECHNOLOGY
Jeff Goldberg/ESTO *photographs*
Mary-Ann Agresti *furniture and furnishings*